D0292153

WITHDRAWN

Books by Penelope Mortimer

FICTION

Long Distance
The Home
My Friend Says It's Bulletproof
The Pumpkin Eater
Saturday Lunch with the Brownings
Daddy's Gone A-hunting (*Cave of Ice* in America)
The Bright Prison
A Villa in Summer
Johanna

NONFICTION

About Time
With Love and Lizards

About Time

About Time AN ASPECT OF AUTOBIOGRAPHY BY *Penelope Mortimer*

1979
DOUBLEDAY & COMPANY, INC.
GARDEN CITY, NEW YORK

Library of Congress Cataloging in Publication Data

Mortimer, Penelope, 1918–
  About time.

  1. Mortimer, Penelope, 1918–   —Biography—Youth.
2. Authors, English—20th century—Biography.
I. Title.
PR6063.O815Z463   1979   823'.9'14 [B]
ISBN: 0-385-08457-9
Library of Congress Catalog Card Number 78-14707

. . . . *though one cannot always*
Remember exactly why one has been happy,
There is no forgetting that one was.

W. H. Auden

Parts of this book are based on material that has appeared in *The New Yorker* under the titles "The Parson," "Curriculum Vitae," "Relatives," and "In the First Place." I would like to thank *The New Yorker*, the Corporation of Yaddo, and all those friends—including my children—whose faith and encouragement persuaded me that it was worth writing.

Penelope Mortimer
June 21, 1978

Contents

Ancestors   13

Father   23

Mother   37

In the First Place   51

In the Second Place   77

Bowerhill   99

In the Third Place   125

In the Fourth Place   135

In the Fifth Place   171

In the Sixth Place   197

Ancestors

Autobiographies or biographies that start with a vast crowd of historical extras always dispirit me. Undoubtedly one's ancestors have a remote bearing on one's life, and an eighteenth-century redhead may throw up a ginger baby in 1980. Beyond that, anything further back than a grandparents' generation seems unnecessary padding, unless there is a wavering line leading back to Shakespeare or a Pope.

Fortunately I know almost nothing about my ancestors and see no particular reason to find out. There is a doubtful story about some Spanish aristocrat or unhappy Moor (which is where the doubt lies) being washed up on the shores of Cornwall during, or after, the Spanish Armada—that would have been on my mother's side and might account for a certain swarthiness in our coloring. And there was a pair of sugar tongs in my father's family which reputedly belonged to Joseph Addison.

Long after that, there was a tribe of Strattons, who produced my maternal grandmother; and a clan of Forbeses, presumably flourishing in kilts and heather, who produced my paternal grandmother. That is quite enough, and the mid-nineteenth century is as far back as I care to go.

Each of my grandmothers bore eleven children. This is one of the few things my father and mother had in common, and with it an early apprenticeship to death. Brothers and sisters died frequently. They were commemorated in cameo brooches, mourning rings, and the ledgers of family Bibles: Constance, William, May, Arthur—all mature ghosts long before I was born. Not only the siblings but the fathers too went early to death, firmly believing that they would gain more health, wealth, and wisdom in the next world. They were both in their graves by the time they were in their mid-forties, leaving about a dozen surviving sons and two wives between them, to carry on the family businesses as best they might.

My knowledge of my paternal grandfather, Robert Jamieson Fletcher, is, like his family's, very sketchy. He was born in 1853 and married Eleanor Jane Forbes, whose father had three successive wives and twenty-two children, seventeen of whom died in infancy. In spite of this drain on his time and energy, he was a successful manufacturing chemist, one of the first exploiters in England of aniline from coal tar, and reasonably wealthy. When he died, he left a large share of his sizable fortune to his daughter Eleanor ("Nellie" to those friends she had), which enabled my grandfather to buy two jewelry shops in the City, both hopelessly unprofitable. Eventually he abandoned them and invested more of his wife's capital in a printing business in Chatham.

It seems he was, in the Victorian manner, *bel homme.* He took his eldest son, Bertie, to Lords in a hansom cab; he smoked expensive cigars and enjoyed his food and drink; he was a fundamentalist in his religious beliefs, and very afraid of my grandmother, who held the purse strings. It's said that he had "good taste"—whatever that was—in books, pictures, and music, and that he had a "beautiful, pure tenor voice"—about the only thing that he was able to bequeath to my father. He died in 1896, when the eldest of the eleven was only nineteen; and as he was always, in life and after it, overpowered by his wife, it isn't surprising that the memories of him are tenuous.

I didn't like my grandmother Nellie. She seemed to me as large, fierce, and demonstrative as my mother's mother was fragile, timid, and remote. Nellie had a sizable wart, or possibly mole, on her left cheek, which I imagined—with the rich disgust I chewed through gristle on the Sunday roast—biting off. It seemed to me that she lived in a poky, dark house, though this was probably because she was the kind of woman who overflowed normal furniture and could have filled a small mansion with her moody presence. The house (Silex, The Grove, Deal, Kent—how many envelopes reluctantly addressed, letters even more reluctantly written?) was probably the usual gloomy, detached Victorian villa, modestly clothed in shrubs. I remember nothing vital about it, such as the kitchen or lavatory, or the room in which I slept on my occasional visits—only the overstuffed drawing room, my grandmother clasping me to some part of herself while I struggled for breath against what may have been bombazine and was certainly whalebone; the anguish transmitted to me where I hid under the table as my father sang the Nunc Dimittis, somberly accompanied by my grandmother on the piano, and I thought he was preparing to die after leaving me in her terrible charge.

There were aunts in this unhappy house: Jessie and

Phyllis. The former, in my memory, was a venomous woman, an energetic chapel-goer, a scrawny, sour creature. Nevertheless, it was Jessie I wrote to from school when I lost my purse; it was Jessie who sent me a ten-shilling note and didn't, as far as I know, tell my father. So she may have been generous and even affectionate; but the way she appeared in my nightmares—of which Silex, The Grove, was one—was as a shrew, a witch, acid-tongued, with glittering ratty eyes and a bundle of old hair.

There was always something faintly daring about Phyllis, my youngest aunt; almost, to my puritanical child's mind, risqué. She seemed to laugh more often than the rest of the family did. I even had the feeling—inexplicable, vaguely troubling—that my brother's attitude toward her was not entirely nephewlike. Perhaps she was pretty. She married, anyway, and in later life became a driving instructress, perpetuating the devil-may-care image, skirts occasionally riding above the knee.

The rest of my father's siblings escaped, in various ways, from my ogre grandmother, their loving mother. Apart from these aunts, and Uncle Bertie, I knew none of them. There was a cousin who may have become a Roman Catholic priest and may have become an expert in ecclesiastical music—I rather hope so. There was Frank, who went to America via Canada and became an American—I remember that he wrote to my father when I was about thirteen, saying that he was now a chief accountant in General Electric and had a large house, two cars, and presumably a family. The letter began (I can see the script now, sloping and orderly), "Hi, you old sky pilot!" My father, appalled, dropped it ostentatiously into the wastepaper basket, from which I'm sure he recovered it the moment he was alone.

And I heard many stories of Jim, who lived a short bad life and came to a bad end, blowing his brains out in Sydney, Australia. When I was about eight years old, what seemed to me then an inordinate number of Jim's children arrived in Deal and shattered the turgid gloom with their unfortunate accents and high spirits. I still preferred them at the time to my other Australian cousins, my mother's nephews and nieces, who dogged my childhood with their dreadful excellence, nobility of soul, and aptitude for mathematics.

My mother's family, the Maggs, came originally—or from the eighteenth century at least, which is far enough back—from the rural coal-mining area of Radstock, in Somerset. The first Charles Maggs, a farmer, was a practical young man who looked around him and saw industry becoming far more profitable than cows. He knew a bit about ropemaking, and rightly believed that there was a profitable connection between rope and the new, booming coal mines. In 1803 he invested his savings in an old cloth mill in Melksham, a great stone castle situated, by its seventeenth-century architect, in fourteen acres along the bank of the canal which would provide my great-great-grandfather with transport, as well as custom for his ropes. He planted trees, to support the great weight of half-mile lengths of taut rope; spinning together through some force which I, well over a century later, could never understand, they made the huge cables, ten inches thick, which would haul coalpit cages up and down deep mine shafts.

Charles Maggs did well, supplying mines and barges all over England, and he thanked God by building Melksham's first Wesleyan chapel and by founding a dynasty. By the time his grandson, my grandfather, was born in 1849, the men of the family were Melksham's elder statesmen, and the women efficiently ordered great staffs of servants from the childbeds in which, for at least half their lives, they were confined.

They were all liberal men; there was no Dickensian squalor in the rope factory; every worker was, in a way, a member of the Maggs family, even if they did sit below the salt. Cottages were provided for them adjoining the workshops, and their children's heads were smooth from kindly patting. The Maggs were austere and generous men who felt respect for God rather than fear, as though He were a senior partner. Their detestation of popery sprang from this respect: Catholicism was foreign, embarrassing, and gaudy with graven images, whereas God, like my grandfather, wore good, sober clothes, a black, hard felt hat with a wide clerical brim and a high crown, a silk topper for special occasions, a Gladstone collar fastened by a single gold stud, and was, with no shadow of doubt, an Englishman.

God and my grandfather headed the crusade for compulsory education in Melksham. Not, they declared, that laborers' children should learn Greek, Latin, algebra, and geometry—no, that would be a waste of time—but a firm grounding in reading, writing, and arithmetic would surely make them *better* laborers than their fathers, and dispel the filthy ignorance on which Romish practices could flourish. Their impassioned views prevailed, and the first Board

School was started in Melksham. In time, my grandfather's gardener's son became headmaster of it; and my grandfather was deprived of a gardener's boy.

He died on November 3, 1898, two days after my mother's birthday, surviving his hero, Gladstone, by only six months. His sons—unlike my father and his wayward brothers—took over all his responsibilities.

They were heavy. When steel cables began increasingly to be used by mines and ships and barges, my grandfather had stepped up the manufacture of cords, twines, tarpaulins and marquees, coir fiber matting. As a sideline, he had begun to exploit the great Wiltshire dairy trade by starting a depot where surplus milk could be turned into butter and cream to be sold in London and other remote cities. This came to be known as the United Dairies, the first organization to sell country products to the cities on a large scale. It was my grandfather's business sense that resulted in all my childhood celebrations, whatever the weather, taking place in tents, and in all my party and Christmas balloons being stamped indelibly with the legend "Diploma Cheese."

"The Dairies" soon became far mightier and more profitable than the rope factory. But in 1898 rope was still the Maggs' major concern, and was therefore bequeathed to the eldest son, Charles William—my Uncle Will. The secondary business, milk, went to Uncle Joe, and soon The Dairies recruited nearly all male descendants, including the women's husbands. The few, like my brother, who rejected the lure of milk were regarded severely as defectors.

Father

My father, the first time I remember him, was dressed in the uniform of Honorary Chaplain to His Majesty's Forces —why, since it must have been peacetime and was certainly summer and therefore nowhere near Armistice Day, I have no idea. Perhaps it was a form of economy, and certainly he would have preferred it to the uniform of cassock, surplice, and dog collar that he was forced to wear on Sundays.

The encounter took place at the end of a long path (where he later built a summerhouse smelling of tar and resin) in the vicarage garden at Chilton. I was in my pram, a lofty vehicle with a fringed awning. I decided—my first conscious decision—to move to the other end of the pram. It capsized. In the general turmoil—I suppose of shock, pain, bewilderment, and the spinning spokes of the pram wheels—I saw my father, in uniform, hurrying down the path toward me. I put this into a novel almost fifty years later, but in the novel my father was blind and passed me by. My father was not blind, and I presume picked me up and made comforting noises. I remember only the decision, the shock, and the smooth khaki twill, wool, or suiting, the handsome Sam Browne belt, the romantic clothes of authority.

Of course he was not like that at all. But that was how he seemed to me at the time, and that was how Mr. W. Riddick, a Melksham photographer, saw him through his lens in about 1920: smiling, cuddling the plump little petticoated girl on his knee, stout legs in laced breeches and golfing socks, a good tweed jacket and waistcoat, a bow tie, a bit of a dandy. Neither I nor Mr. Riddick ever mistook him for a man of God.

I think he was a clergyman for one reason only—there was nothing else, as Nellie Fletcher's second son, he could possibly have been. As a small boy, bullied and teased by six sisters and four brothers, he sat under the nursery table chanting, "Mama, Papa, all the children are disagreeable except me," to the tune of "Gentle Jesus." The Almighty shone a compassionate eye through the silk tassels on the green serge tablecloth, disregarded the ten clever goody-goodies, and picked him out. He began preaching—a stocky, timid, bombastic little boy shouting of hell-fire in the front parlor while his brother Bertie sneered and his sisters tittered and his father played the harmonium. As a reward, his grandmother would give him lollipops, lovingly slipped from her tongue onto his. The only color in the house was the white of the girls' petticoats whisking round dark corners.

He went to various schools, but learned nothing. He was beaten, put in the attic, kept on bread and water. This made him cry, convinced him that he was a sinner, but made him even more stupid. At sixteen, hair slicked down from a center parting, stiff-collared, in dog's-tooth check, he was taken away from school and bound as an apprentice in my grandfather's printing firm. The other apprentices were disagreeable; he clung firmly to his parents' Nonconformist God and became a preacher in the local Wesleyan chapel, flaying the nodding bonnets with his great new voice, guiltily and savagely in love with a girl named Minnie Minnie, bobbish, rich, fifteen, was frightened and ran away; she never married, but became a close friend of my mother's and at some point in my childhood set up a cake shop (it was called The Confiserie) in Gerrards Cross with a gaunt lady called Margaret. Her startled giggle, her look of petrified alarm, were surely caused by my father's adolescent passion. She was one of the many single women in my childhood whom I had to call Aunt. Aunt Margaret and Aunt Minnie always made my birthday cakes, and I remember them as the smell of chocolate icing and the touch of greaseproof paper. When Minnie looked at me, she probably thanked the grace of God.

Back in the early 1900s, my grandfather died, the printing firm collapsed. Browbeaten or entreated (the same thing, I suspect) by my grandmother, my father enrolled in a Wesleyan Theological College in Richmond.

It was a ghastly mistake. Black-suited, forced to attend long lectures on the Roman baptismal creed, to puzzle his way through Athanasius and Marcellus and the Cappadocians, to battle with the theory of enhypostasia and Socinianism and kenosis, to listen to pale young men with clammy hands discussing Theodore of Mopsuestia and the laws of ecclesiastical polity—all this was the nearest thing to hell he had ever known. God moved away from him. For the first time in his life, with the agony of a child who sees his father pinching the maid's bottom, he had Doubts. He wept and prayed, but it was no good. The college expelled him for failing all his examinations. He thought, as he walked slowly away with his Gladstone bag and his Bible, of walking straight on into the placid river; it was the beginning of a clumsy flirtation with suicide that was to last all his life and never be consummated. My grandmother drummed her fingers; he became a Unitarian.

He could preach again, and when he was preaching he could convince himself of anything. He shook his square hands, howled and whispered; his huge, resonant voice shook the corrugated-iron roofs of dismal chapels, stroked the souls of girls in village halls. But afterward, alone in his lodging, he suffered. Preaching, although he always worked very hard on his sermons, didn't take up much time. He had begun to read Nietzsche and, almost more furtively, H. G. Wells; he had heard, uneasily, of "Man and Superman," and the phrase "life-force" began to creep into his sermons. The idea of Life, which had nothing to do with living, had begun to take the place of God, who had shown Himself to have nothing to do with religion. "Life is Love!" he bawled to a startled congregation. Pinchmouthed, severely buttoning their gloves, they asked him to leave. He packed his *Zarathustra* and left.

What to do with him now? He was twenty-eight, uneducated, unqualified, tormented by the sins he hadn't committed and unable to understand the ones he had; tremendously ambitious, without the slightest talent for success; full of urges and yearnings and pains of the soul, frightening and frightened and altogether a mess. The family

bought him a piece of land in the middle of Manitoba and
sent him off, with his brother Frank, to Canada. Perhaps,
as the ship heaved off into the Liverpool fog, they thought
they had seen the last of him.

He never found the piece of land. Perhaps he didn't really look. He took various trains in the hope of finding it,
but always ended up sitting on his trunk in some desolate
halt, waiting for a train to take him back to Winnipeg.
After several of these excursions he gave up and took a job
in a printing firm. It was cold, barbaric. Everyone was disagreeable. He spent hours every night reading Browning out
loud to himself to keep his accent pure. Away from any
form of recognizable religion, his doubts were calmed; the
longer he stayed a printer, the firmer his faith became.
After a year of it, he wrote home for his passage money.
His cold, ink-stained fingers could hardly hold the pen. "I
know," he wrote, "that God intends me for the Ministry."

My grandmother flew into one of her rages, whistled
"Worthy Is the Lamb" under her breath, and sent my
aunts cowering to their rooms. But she was lonely. All her
sons had left her and, with this one exception, were living
brash and ungodly lives, both in jail and out. Bertie was a
cynic; Frank, who had accompanied my father to Canada,
had just killed a lumberman in an argument and temporarily disappeared. She sent the passage money.

So my father came home, chilly, chastened, and full of
hope. He would study, he would do what he was told.
Somebody must want him. Somebody must recognize his
ability. As he set foot on English soil at Liverpool, he felt
that one blast of his voice would be enough. "Why,"

bishops would ask each other, "has he been neglected so long?"

Six months later, in a tweed hat and knickerbockers, he was bicycling about the lanes of Wiltshire, his heavy head bent low over the handlebars, big legs numbly pedaling. He was an itinerant preacher again. Browning went with him everywhere, and his text was always the same: "'Tis not what man does which exalts him, but what man would do!" He arrived in Melksham, and was asked to lunch by my grandmother Charlotte. My mother, handsome, mysteriously ailing, a spinster in her early thirties, delayed going downstairs, dreading yet another sanctimonious suitor. When she saw his tweed hat on the hall chair, her heart (I suppose) turned over a little. When he read "Saul" aloud in the drawing room I was, like it or not, on my way.

He was ready to marry. As I write that, the phrase makes me flinch. A rampaging river, pent up for thirty years, is ready to burst its banks, uproot trees, shatter drawing rooms and nurseries; and my mother, possibly with a parasol, possibly reading *The Life of Buddha*, certainly with a deep distaste for human frailty, sits neatly in a nearby meadow, glancing up from time to time to see that the buttercups are in order and all well. He was ready to marry. She struggled a little, but he got her (she, describing it, said, "We finally made the plunge") early in the morning of Shrove Tuesday, February 8, 1910, in the village church of North Newton, which was very old. They had to walk to the ceremony, and back to her brother Fred's house, across frozen muddy fields, and went off to a predictably disastrous honeymoon in lodgings at Bournemouth.

Fourteen years later, I would begin to know quite a bit

about my father's sex life. In 1910 nobody knew anything; or, more accurately, nobody dared to admit, even to themselves, that they knew anything. But it is obvious that marriage, far from calming him, goaded him into a kind of fury. Ever since Minnie, and probably long before, he had been violently, if furtively, conscious of sex; now, legitimately sexual, he became intoxicated with the idea that the world was more or less equally divided into men and women. Free love and the life-force and the emancipation of women all whirled together in his innocent head, causing an extraordinary chaos in which women were exactly like men and yet were at the same time accessible. His heart gave out under the strain. He became ill. My mother came as near as she could to a nervous breakdown. The Wesleyans turned him out. My mother's family, stern materialists who believed devoutly in success, refused to have anything to do with him. There seemed, this time, no escape.

But of course there was. All his life he had been beating his head against the narrow limits of Nonconformity. The Church of England, that great, placid, unshakable compromise, loomed calm and radiant over the horizon. Why had he never thought of it before? The gracious, socially acceptable vicarages; the brown, book-lined studies where even a heretic could sleep undisturbed; the vast cathedrals that could ring with his reading of Isaiah, of which he was rightly proud; and above all, the limitless scope for a man of talent. Revived, with passionate energy and pin-bright faith, he went off to Lambeth Palace and the Archbishop of Canterbury.

The first question he was asked was whether he had any

money. None. Oxford or Cambridge? Neither. Who would speak for him? No one. A fortnight later a letter came from the Palace, signed with one spidery name: He was not, it was thought, suitable for the Church of England.

Now it was a case of do or die. Browning was no longer any use to him; neither was the life-force. He was well into his thirties, and God was passing him by. He badgered, he pestered, he wrote long, impassioned letters. For the first time in his life he studied, swallowing great chunks of doctrine and not daring to think how uneasily it lay. The end— the refuge with its armchair and the mellow peal of bells— was all that mattered. When at last they accepted him, he wept for joy, although with the appearance of awful grief. Once in the Church, he knew, nothing short of murder or flagrant adultery would get him out.

They gave him the job of curate at Custom House, in the East End of London. They lived, he and my mother, in a little semidetached house (for some curious reason she distastefully called it a villa) next to the gasworks; lascars prowled the streets at night and the church was a grimy great place with a sparse scattering of old women who wanted to take the weight off their feet and get away for an hour or two from their drunken husbands. My father found himself looking with hostile envy at the local Catholic priest—but of course it was too late for that, and far too late for celibacy. He had little interest in saving souls, and none of the parishioners had heard of Browning. My mother applied her skills to visiting the sick, whom my father found intensely disagreeable.

However, London had something to be said for it. He

went, having carefully removed his dog collar, to a private performance of *Mrs. Warren's Profession*; he got to know a few vaguely literary personalities—the humble outer fringe of the Café Royal World; he began to write himself, pouring out his untidy feelings on life and sex and God in dull, pompous sentences to which my mother listened with an expression of hopeless martyrdom that eventually, in his presence, became permanent. For her, as a curate's wife, there had begun the lifelong task of keeping up appearances; she had a great aptitude for this, but I believe that once alone with my father she became quite silent, an industrious shadow, locked and bolted against attack.

But he attacked, nevertheless. He sat on the edge of her bed and talked for hours about spiritual passion, and then he raped her. Not, of course, that he knew what else to do; neither did she. In this abysmal way she conceived for the first time, and had a painful miscarriage on the sofa (Was it a girl? If only it had been a girl, and had survived . . .), and my father began to realize that marriage, far from liberating him, was a terrible trap in which love could only mean damage. The doctors said that she must be taken away from London, that she couldn't survive. I'm sure she pooh-poohed them, but I'm sure everyone believed it. So my father took a locum-tenancy at Ellesborough, in Buckinghamshire, where I have never been, and of which I am obscurely jealous.

Perhaps because I think they may have been happy there. It must have seemed permanent, for my father started to build a bungalow, which they called ("Prophetic, alas!" my mother sighed) Long Hazard. I cannot in any way imagine them living in a bungalow called Long Hazard. In any case, the rector died, and when a new one was appointed, my father—who probably spent more time on the building site than he did in church—got the sack, or whatever courteous means of disposal the Church of England uses for troublesome clergymen.

My mother went through the small print in *The Church Times* and found St. Mary's, Chilton, in Oxfordshire. The village—a cozy huddle of cottages under a gentle, sheltering hill—suited her perfectly. The squire's mansion faced serenely away from the church in its wilderness of moon daisies. The vicarage was quiet in the sun, protected by a high pink wall—a house full of dark passages and damp stone, mellow with dust and the smell of rotting apples. There was no sound but the swing of milk pails carried on their wooden yoke, the clop of a lazy horse, the hum of a fat bee in the honeysuckle. It was hard to keep awake, and a beautiful place to die in—the Church of England at its best.

My father was offered the living, and burst in like a lion. But he hardly had time to scatter the teacups or scythe the daisies—my brother was born almost immediately and then, thank God, came the war, the Great War, the war that gave him his uniform, the war I never knew. He was off in a flash of khaki and leather to become a chaplain, and some old man was installed in Chilton to pray for victory. My mother followed him to Matlock, and then to Woolwich, where the gunfire made the baby cry. At last he was sent overseas, and my mother settled down to a great peace with her son, visiting her family and her (by now) friends Minnie and Margaret. "Overseas" meant, I think, France and Salonika, but either my father didn't tell many stories about the war, or had forgotten them by the time I was old enough to listen, or kept them, unlike the rest of his pain, to himself. I imagine and hope that in those far-off places, with shells bursting and haystacks burning and bits of men strewing the barbed wire, he found some kinds of satisfaction.

He must have come home on leave around Christmas 1917, for by February my mother knew that she was pregnant again. She was forty-two, and not delighted. In the summer, she took a house in Rhyl, near her old friend Florence Hiley, where I was born. I weighed over ten pounds and (she told me frequently) nearly finished her off.

My father came back and we (I suppose I must now write "we") returned to Chilton. The church shook with Isaiah and the moon daisies were scythed down. He persuaded the squire that what was needed was a Village Club, a place where they could come together as a community and live a little. He helped to build it, slapping on the cement—braces straining over his great shoulders, singing at the top of his voice. It was a very ugly building, a gabled and stuccoed monstrosity among the thatched cottages and rosy brick, but the villagers obediently used it, playing slow games of billiards, drinking their pints in a bar as cheerless as a railway refreshment room.

The Church of England had, at last, come up to his expectations—he had a beautiful vicarage, a book-lined study with a comfortable armchair, a thirteenth-century church in which he could cry, "Prepare ye the way of the Lord, make straight in the desert a highway!"; he had a son and a daughter and 250 pounds a year. There was only one thing wrong, apart from the fact his wife wouldn't go near him. He no longer believed in God.

Not only did he no longer believe in God—he didn't believe in the Thirty-nine articles, the Virgin Birth, the idea of the Trinity, the Resurrection, the sacraments, the sanctity of marriage, or the concept of original sin. All that was left was a terror of the hell inside his own head.

He began desperately to try to fill the emptiness. His faith in Life became almost fanatical: loving Life and living Love—the only salvation. If anyone were foolish enough to ask him exactly what it meant, his eyes blazed more fiercely than ever, he flung his arms wide and shouted, "You ask me what Life means? Life! Life speaks for itself!"

But it didn't. He was thirty-nine at the time he held me, petticoated in *broderie anglais,* on his knee to have our photograph taken; the loneliness that had threatened him ever since he hid under the nursery table was already incurable. It would be absurd to pretend that I knew, then, what he was like; it would be equally absurd to pretend, now, that I can't imagine what he was like. My Daddy: and I want to add, the poor sod. But that is because I am older now than he was when we posed in Mr. Riddick's studio, and much wiser. The truth is that I never thought poor sod until long after he was dead, and that has no place in this story.

Mother

My mother was born into a commode on November 1, 1876—All Saints' Day—and all my churchgoing childhood I thought that when we sang "For all thy Saints, who from their labors rest . . ." it was in some way a birthday song for my mother, who rested for exactly one hour every afternoon and ten hours each night under a comfy eiderdown. For the remaining thirteen she sped about like a fly, so that for a while we gave her an onomatopoeic nickname, "Bizzier."

It always sounded to me as though she had a wonderfully happy childhood. Charles Maggs may have been austere, unapproachable, and unsentimental, but he was, according to my mother, deeply affectionate. I'm not quite sure how she knew this, but since she assumed it to be true, it probably was. Not content with eight sons, he called his three daughters—Jenny and May and my mother Amy (after Amy Robsart)—by boys' names: Jack and Tom and Tim. My father called my mother Tim all his life, and I never thought it unsuitable.

As small girls, Jenny/Jack and my mother had their hair cropped; only Tom/May, who was to fade away in her teens, was allowed tresses. In a photograph taken about 1884 (this time by a Mr. Hayward of Devises), ten surviv-

ing children face the camera unsmiling in front of the veranda at Bowerhill: My mother, in button boots, looking a
little hobbledehoy, holds a large straw hat on her lap;
Tom/May grasps an unlikely tennis racket; the little boys
wear sailor suits, the older ones strike poses vaguely reminis-
cent of Nelson. My grandfather looks pleased with himself,
my grandmother both shy and intrepid. It is hard to imagine them as live people, or the chatter and bustle they must
have broken into when Mr. Hayward had finished his job,
the children swarming over the garden or given back to
nursemaids. In some way the lack of noise in the picture is
more curious than the lack of movement.

At Christmas the Town Band came and played carols in
the garden at midnight, reducing my mother to pleasurable
tears; in the summer there were tennis parties, a marquee
(stamped, as mine were, with the huge name of Maggs)
set up in the orchard for the boy visitors. They played I
Spy in the dark garden, Kickory (a kind of hide-and-seek)
at night, and charades. My mother climbed the same trees
and walls, paddled in the same brook that I was to splash
about in over forty years later. They piled into horse-drawn
brakes and took picnics to Longleat, Laycock Abbey, and
Savernake Forest. My mother looked after her doll's pram
by washing it with milk and made herself a home in the
apple loft, where she concocted salads of buttercup roots,
and jelly out of sorrel leaves. She rode a staid pony called
Amorous until she learned to control Topsy; in later years
she hafted Topsy to a dog cart and tore about the Wiltshire lanes, getting herself known as "Miss Jehu." Bicycling
was only permitted for the girls if they wore special skirts

made by the local tailor, dark gray, with elastic stirrups to
keep them decent at such reckless speed.

But there was no indulgence: When my mother hid in
the high cow parsley to avoid lessons, she was punished by
being shut in the spare room, where the children's Sunday
clothes, which they hated, were always laid out in readiness
on the four-poster bed. There was no talking at meals, and
the girls sat strapped to backboards to improve their pos-
ture. Cake appeared only on Sundays, and attendance at
family prayers was obligatory every day of the week, the
rows of children and maids and visitors listening to my
grandfather with bowed heads and scuffling knees. The
girls and the smaller boys were all made to work for good
causes: They picked and sold blackberries to send mis-
sionaries overseas, knitted and crocheted for orphans and
soldiers and the destitute, delivered home-made pies and
jellies to the sick and needy. Every day my grandfather
would tell them, "What does the Lord require of thee but
to do justly, love mercy, and walk humbly with thy God."
This appears to have been a statement rather than a question, but the additional requirement must have been to
cultivate a good business sense and make as much honest
money as possible.

And there were mysteries: My mother's first memory
was of waking in a cot that had perforated tin sides (by no
stretch of the imagination could it have been the commode?) and the thousands of tiny holes sang "For ever and
ever" and didn't stop however loudly she screamed. I am
by no means sure, knowing my mother a little, that they
were warning her that she would live for ninety-six years,

which is as near ever as makes no difference. However, her stern parents took her into their room for comfort. She obviously didn't remember this when I woke with a child's nightmare, for she told me to go back to bed and think about my dolls. What, I wondered even then, can you *think* about dolls?

But she had some method of quickening them, those lifeless images of china or—in my day—celluloid, with their uncanny blinking eyes that shut with a little click, the lashes thick and smooth on the cold faces. They were alive to her, because they died: broke, revealing awful hollows and sockets, chubby limbs hinged with rubber bands, ghastly rosebud smiles (the parted lips, the glimpse of milk teeth) unchanged on their decapitated heads; worst of all, to my mother, the glass eyes of a dead, dismembered doll— even in my childhood, she couldn't look at them. Her favorite brother, Joe, chased her round the house with a pair of them; she slammed a door on him, screaming, and the latch cut his forehead open. Her punishment was to go to the doctor with him and watch the cut being sewn up; to endure his stoicism.

They had governesses who, for some reason, were "inadequate," and at thirteen my mother was sent to boarding school, first in Marlborough, then in Weston-super-Mare. (This is curious, since girls were not normally sent away to school; but perhaps my grandfather believed in educating women, as well as the laboring classes.) My mother won a medal for gymnastics and left school in the summer before her seventeenth birthday with a quotation from the ubiquitous Mr. Browning written in her autograph book by her favorite teacher: "The common problem, yours, mine, everyone's, is not to fancy what were fair in life provided it *might* be, but finding what *is*, then find how to make that fair up to our means—a very different thing." She took it to heart, where in time she stowed away some tenets of Eastern philosophy and theosophy and lived on it, like a camel off its hump, for the rest of her life.

Perhaps, instead of returning home, she should have galloped into the Middle East, organized a Scutari or poured out, high on some crag or moor, the dark secrets of her strong soul and head; she should at least, at some time in her life, have chained herself to a railing. Instead, obedient to her provincial Victorian upbringing, she became a missionary to a small, inaccessible hamlet called Redstocks, a mile or so across the fields. There was no road to it, and the villagers, inbred, illiterate, living in squalor and violence, were in far greater need of enlightenment than any African tribe heating up cauldrons for gospelers. My mother, at the age of seventeen, took them on single-handed, galoshing her way through the mud with bundles of tracts, not necessarily religious but always uplifting, and generous supplies of calf's-foot jelly.

Dickens had been dead for over twenty years, but had inspired no reforms in Redstocks. In order to endure at all, the villagers were well stocked up with penny pints of ale and gin, existing in an alcoholic stupor enlivened only by brawls and punch-ups and murder. My mother was given the use of a mission room furnished with a harmonium, a few rows of pews, and a smoky Tortoise stove. She started Mothers' Meetings, a Sunday school, evening clubs where

she taught them macramé—a kind of coarse lacemaking—
and nets for presumably quite useless hammocks; she organized "Socials," and theatricals for the children. She
even taught them a humane method of snaring rabbits.
One evening a virago burst into the hall, brandishing a
plate of charred fried potato. "Look, miss," she demanded,
"isn't that enough supper for him? I was only singing
'What is home without a mother' and he came for me with
the poker. He said, 'I'd kill you but you ain't worth hanging for,' and I ain't going home unless you comes with me,
miss!" My mother was always a small woman, and must
have been what was known as a wisp of a girl; but a photograph of her at that time shows steady, bold eyes and a de-
termined mouth on which a smile hovers like an unnecessary decoration. She probably scolded the fellow roundly,
sobered him up with a pot of strong tea, and started him
on his way to becoming an exemplary citizen.

These were the best stories I heard in my childhood:
Three-year-old Gladys, swinging on a gate, leg on each side
of it, was horribly squashed between the gate and the gate-
post. As she lay mangled and dying, the child called pit-
eously for a mug of ale. Her mother, "reading penny novel-
ettes" in the corner, took no notice, and when Gladys was
dead she was thrown into the coal shed. One day my
mother was tending to a dying man who moaned repeatedly
for his wife, who was out in the yard plucking chickens—
"You get on with your dyin'," the good wife yelled, "and
I'll get on with my pluckin'!" But my favorite was the one
about the witch who lived in a derelict thatched cottage
and who according to my mother, was "a very rough and

blasphemous old crone," regarded with superstitious terror
by the villagers. When she, too, was dying, my mother visited her every day. For some reason, she thought the old
hag should die clean; she tried to wash her with soap and
water, but the dirt was so ingrained that she had to scrub it
off with turpentine. When the carcass was more or less
respectable for death, my mother turned her attention to
the windows, so overgrown with cobwebs and filth that
inside the cottage was perpetual night. The old woman
bounced up, outraged. "Don't you do that, miss, or the
angels'll come flyin' in, them's beatin' their wings on the
panes already!" Then she gave my mother a rather beautiful ladder-back chair, lay back, and privately, safely hidden
from the avenging angels, drifted into death.

At night, when her work was over, my mother would be
escorted back across the fields by a young farm laborer
called Jim Helps. He was drunk most of the day, but always sobered up in the evenings to walk my mother home.
On her birthday, the whole of Redstocks was invited to a
party with fireworks and a huge bonfire in the orchard.
(Was she imperious, merry, did she dance with Jim?)

She was, although she may not have realized it, extremely attractive: small-boned, with elegant legs and delicate hands, a heavy heap of dark brown hair—I remember
when she had it bobbed or shingled, and the long, thick
plaits of dead hair were kept in tissue paper for years.
There must have been many young men who hankered
after her, but she resisted them all, including a curate who
proposed by telling her fervently that she was the kind of
girl he wanted to weep over his coffin at his funeral. She

was severely reprimanded for putting her head under the
green baize behind the local photographer's camera, while
he showed her how to adjust the lens. Her father and
brothers were everywhere; there was no room for any more
men.

After my grandfather died, my mother began a long
series of illnesses, anemia, rheumatic fever, abscesses, ery-
thema, probably most of them symptoms of a rebellious
and frustrated spirit. The local doctor told her to wear a
blue ribbon and live on onions, so she was taken to a Sir
William Broadment in Harley Street, who prescribed two
months in Switzerland. She refused to leave until Joe, already prospering in milk, had offered to pay for a dea-
conness to carry on in Redstocks. Then she obediently
went to Zermatt with her mother and her Aunt Maria, and
walked in the mountains and picked eidelweiss and took
photographs and was very homesick. This must have been
about the time when my father was thinking of throwing
himself in the Thames.

She came back, apparently restored, to Bowerhill and
Redstocks. But something was wrong (her father and
William Gladstone were dead, the oil paintings of both of
them just stared and stared day after day). She went for a
long visit to her brother Joe, who was living in Hampstead.

In Worsley Road she met, for the first time, a touch of
sophistication: There may even have been a freethinker or
two among the medical students and young businessmen;
she might have been taken to see Sarah Bernhardt or Si-
gnora Duse at the Adelphi or Mrs. Patrick Campbell doing
her *Second Mrs. Tanquery* at the New Theatre or Miss

Marie Tempest in *Caste* at the Criterion. But although she always talked of this visit as though it had been a golden time, a kind of honeymoon, the obscure rashes and fevers continued. Joe brought in a nerve specialist, Arthur John Whiting, who fell heavily and gloomily in love.

The affair, or engagement, lasted three years. Dr. Whiting was obviously a manic-depressive, unable to heal himself, and my mother was unable to cope with his "moods," having been taught that virtue was the sole cause of happiness and sin of depression. He would lock himself away for days at a time, then turn up full of wit and sparkle; she would give a Dr. Jekyll some letters to post, but by the time he reached the front door a distraught Mr. Hyde would post them back into her own letter box. Whenever they settled on a date for the wedding, he would become speechless with misery. He consulted an old friend, a clergyman, who told him that the best cure was marriage; but by this time my mother had decided that she wouldn't be a human sacrifice, however worthy the cause. She broke off the engagement and was taken by her mother to Norway, where Ibsen, driven mad by the nineteenth century, was about to die.

I doubt whether she had been with Joe to see Miss Ellen Terry in *The Vikings* or whether she ever knew of Hedda Gabler or Rebecca West. If she had, she might have recognized the part of herself that only piped up occasionally in the characters of Tim or Jehu. Already a spinster (she was nearly thirty), her companion on this trip was her old schoolfriend, Flo Hiley, the one who lived in Rhyl and who would become my brother's godmother and, for a short while, my headmistress. My grandmother presumably sat and looked at the fjords while "the girls" went sailing and walking with a dashing Mr. Aldred, the owner of the hotel, and a lugubrious Norwegian professor who attached himself to Flo but unfortunately lost his hold on her. Shortly before it was time to leave, their ship, the *Midsummer Sun*, wired to say that the weather had broken and the return voyage was canceled. Panic, cast away on some foreign shore, fluttering despair: but Mr. Aldred was in command of the shipping lines, if not the elements, and a dreadful German steamer called by to pick them up. The voyage took two weeks of horrible discomfort, continuous seasickness: By the time they stepped ashore my mother wished she had married the unstable Dr. Whiting and stayed at home.

So she was again living at Bowerhill, and the visiting preachers came and went. Once the weather cleared, Mr. Aldred lost no time in traveling to Melksham to pay court; but my mother turned him down—to my regret, since I can't help feeling that the Maggs part of me would have been happy to have a Norwegian hotelier as a father. She decided to go to Sesame, a small training college in London, to learn how to look after babies. Her six months there were happy and instructive but apparently purposeless, since at the end of them she went home again, with no babies to look after.

Two years passed before my father came to lunch in his tweed hat. I don't know what she thought or felt or did. It obviously never occurred to Will or Joe to teach her about rope or milk; although there was a strong tradition of unmarried women in the family, she was too conditioned in her role of daughter and sister to strike out on her own; she assumed that she needed a man to take care of her, although it was the last thing she wanted, unless the man happened to be a Maggs. She was always very obstinate, and even if she had known someone who might have tried to argue her into independence, she would have won the argument by retreating into a stubborn silence that would be softened by only the faintest hint of martyrdom, the faintest smile of a soul suffering fools gladly. She needed someone who believed in Eno's Fruit Salts and cold baths and a brisk walk to work before breakfast. The last person in the world she needed was Arthur Forbes Gerard Fletcher, five years her junior, a foreigner from Deal.

In the First Place

1

The first place I remember is the vicarage, Chilton, near Thame, Oxon. (an abbreviation of Oxfordshire which always perplexed me and still does). As far as I know, I never wrote a letter to this address, since I never left it without my parents. But letters must have arrived—from my brother, away at school, perhaps? I certainly never read one, but as in those days children were forced to write home every Sunday, I realize that he must have written. Perhaps—an extraordinary thought—he was told to send me his love.

My brother had been born in Chilton, which, I always felt uneasily, gave him a prior claim to it. This was illogical, because he didn't seem to live there. For the four years before my birth, our mother lavished all her love and care on him; she wrote "The Future Prime Minister!" under a photograph of him standing unsteadily on a lawn; she had smocked his linen smocks and written down every move he made in a big freckled notebook. Then, when she was pregnant with me, she sent him away to boarding school. He was four years old, and he never came back.

Oh, there was a moody figure, a kind of small, embodied tension around in the school holidays. There is an oval,

sepia photograph of a small boy holding a teddy bear and
smiling at a pretty nurse, who holds me. I remember a red
tape tied around a child's gray flannel sleeve after a small-
pox vaccination, and later I heard about academic bril-
liance and scholarships and shining hopes for his future.
But the memories I have of him at Chilton are like the mo-
ments when a shadow suddenly seems to solidify and take
some recognizable, usually threatening, shape. I didn't realize for years how much—whether he knew it or not—he
must hate me, connecting my birth with his exile. I only
remember the times when he tricked or tortured me, and
that I felt my wails of indignation were righteous. I'm surprised, in fact, that he let me live at all.

Why she did this terrible thing to him is a mystery. My
father, off in some remote trench or writing letters for illiterate Tommies in Salonika, couldn't have been responsible.
The only possible explanation is that she hoped, if my
brother could become extremely taciturn, learn to play
cricket and tennis, rugger and golf (which was always pronounced "goff"), get infected with high principles and acceptable morals, that he might—being second in the line of
succession—become Heir to the Milk Kingdom. It was
therefore unthinkable (to her) to send him to the village
school, to learn his three R's with the laboring classes; and
although Thame, Aylesbury, and even Oxford were perfectly accessible, she must have believed that there was
something about boarding school that would produce an
added strength of character, even in a four-year-old. Also
the sons of the local gentry, though slightly older, were
being sent away to become, in another half a century,

judges and lord chamberlains and speakers of the House. Perhaps she thought that if my brother toddled in these illustrious footsteps he might, in time, "get to know the right people." Perhaps she didn't want him corrupted by the Fletchers, who had unstable attitudes, unsuitable for a growing boy. I don't know; and when I taxed her with it in later years, neither did she.

I am sure that she missed him dreadfully, and sent him incessant letters and cakes and pairs of sturdy combinations, which, in time, yellowed and darned, would be passed on to me, along with his outgrown gray flannel shorts. Their closest contact must have been through the village postman, who collected, as well as delivered, all communications.

The village postman had been blown up in some horrible way in the Great War: His face was a formless red and purple mishmash with five hollow apertures and no nose. He didn't frighten me in the least, and must have had a kindly nature. He wore a blue uniform with gold buttons. In those days postmen, milkmen, bus conductors and drivers, all railwaymen, and, of course, chauffeurs wore uniforms. So did the district nurse on her energetic bicycle. It was easy to identify people, and to tell which side they were on. The squire of the village, who was in the Guards, was frequently resplendent as a Christmas tree, topped with a huge bearskin. All maids, however young or friendly with their employers, wore dark dresses and white aprons and cotton caps. My nurse wore a veil like a nun and a starched collar like a businessman. The phrase "in mufti" was still used, implying that everyone had a uniform to put on for suitable occasions, and that their ordinary clothes were intended, like pajamas, for relaxation.

The village of Chilton was—and still is—haphazard, mainly consisting of a thirteenth-century church on a hill, a vast Queen Anne manor, the exquisite dower house at its gate—where the schoolmaster, a Mr. Ambrose, lived—a couple of farms, and the vicarage. There was a blacksmith (the smell of singeing hooves is powerfully nostalgic as the smell of paraffin) and a village shop, which was the front room of a small, dark cottage—a jumble of boot laces, pencils, and boiled sweets, in which Mrs. Jessup, a doubled-up old witch no taller than myself, crouched behind the counter, alert as a crab. Until my father built his Village Club, there was no pub for at least a mile. There were a few what my mother disparagingly referred to as "council houses" (which I suppose they were, but she made them sound almost immoral), in one of which lived a family called Hubbard. There were a great many young, friendly Hubbards, but I was seldom allowed to play with them, and then only in the vicarage garden.

The vicarage was—is—one of those serene, modestly beautiful houses that could never have been newly built (and yet think of the din there must have been in those parts through the Middle Ages and up to the eighteenth century—the hammering and sawing, cranking and hauling, half-built churches littering the hillsides, manors and mansions rising out of rubble, incessant industry where now there is only architecture). Some ruthless Victorian parson with twelve children had slapped a hideous gabled appendage onto the side of it, and that, for a few of my first eight years, housed the dormitory and schoolroom for my mother's Residential Nursery, which she whimsically called the Little People's Garden. Before this shrewd or willful venture, my father's bedroom was in the gabled wing; during it, he left home and lived in a restored army hut in the orchard. As the orchard was on the other side of the road from the house and garden, I didn't so much see my father as visit him or meet him accidentally. Therefore, according to my convictions at the time—which were loosely based on Bishop Berkeley's doctrine that matter as an unperceived substance is both impossible and unreal—he seldom existed.

If I try to evoke him, he comes in fits and starts, like a poorly received spirit. He frightened me. He laid a spaniel puppy on its back and showed me its genitals, but I don't know what the dog was called, and nobody loved it. He performed in church, strangely dressed in skirts. He built me a house in the trees, he built me a doll's house. He may have exposed himself to me once, in an upstairs room; I don't think I ever saw him entirely naked. On one of my early birthdays he constructed a very ingenious obstacle race on the tennis lawn, and on this same lawn he once played a game with me called, he said, "Tread on the tail of my coat," which consisted in him running about for a little while trailing a blanket, which I was supposed to jump on and capture. And one Christmas he, or he and my mother, or he and my mother and governess, or—more likely—he and my governess, turned the whole dining room into a dark but glinting cave, with an enormous cracker, dangling presents, slung from the ceiling; and in a firelit

corner my father, dressed as a witch (not Santa Claus—but
why not Santa Claus?), stirring a cauldron of yet more
presents while inappropriately chanting (in his church
voice), "Double, double, toil and trouble, fire burn and
cauldron bubble. . . ." I was terrified, and burst into tears,
but could not explain why.

He drove a Morris Oxford and allowed me to ride astride
the hood, which burned the insides of my thighs. Once,
when he had gone to London for the day, I listened with
my ear to the ground like an American Indian to hear the
car coming back from fifty miles away; but didn't hear it.
He showed me a book of female anatomy, in which a flap
opened over the womb, revealing a very small, ugly, upside-
down fetus; but I thought it was rather a beautiful book.
He played tennis in the summer, and goff in the right season, and was often in a bad temper, once throwing my
brother out of the dining room window, which was all of
two feet above a bed of wallflowers.

I remember even less about my mother in those early
years. She was always busy cooking or gardening, hurrying
about. Sometimes we may have played Up Jenkins or Hunt
the Thimble. She sent me off to tea at the squire's mansion, grizzling and reluctant, a clean handkerchief tucked
into my knickers. She took me to church on Sunday morn-
ings, though always let me go before the sermon. During
the week, I sometimes went with her and pottered about
while she arranged the altar flowers or changed the frontal
or hung up a clean surplice for my father or checked the
supplies of blood and body. She loved to decorate the
church, and did it with no sense of religion at all: At

Christmas only ("No popery" was written on her heart) there were candles, at Easter every white and yellow flower or blossom she could lay hands on; at Harvest Festival her imagination ran riot with vegetables and fruit, Michaelmas daisies and wheat, so that altar, pulpit, choir stalls, lectern, and font looked like exhibits at a county fair. Until the start of the Little People's Garden, I connect my mother only with rooms and with things, colors and furniture and food. She must have spoken; but my impression is that the sound of her voice didn't reach me.

The rooms she furnished were, like the church she decorated, made very much her own. My mother had collected furniture all her life, scrounging about in woodsheds and dairies, finding treasures. Most of it was made of fruit woods, though there was also oak and walnut and a few strictly simple pieces of mahogany. She had a weakness for chintz, but the designs were never fussy; basically she was a burlap woman, and indulged in linen—William Morris browns and plums and terra cottas—on the rare occasions when she could afford it. Unlike all the other vicarages I was to visit in my childhood, my homes had no religious pictures or emblems on their white—or, at their most flamboyant, pale primrose—walls, except, perhaps, for a Margaret Tarrant in the nursery, a Rosetti print on the back stairs; they were not lit by dismal forty-watt bulbs hanging from dingy ceilings, were never icy with poverty, never smelled of last Sunday's boiled cabbage. For the hardy, pioneering little woman my mother seemed to be, she had a great appreciation of comfort. The mattress on her bed was always of a make called Vi-spring; she had a

rubber hot-water bottle when the rest of us had to make do
with stone ones; there was always a mohair rug available
to tuck around her knees in a draft. She was extremely, but
unobtrusively, economical; because of her talent for finding
out what *was*, then finding out how to make that fair up
to her means, I never believed my parents were poor.

They didn't, of course, own a wall or roof or inch of
land, and never had—except for what I prefer to believe
was the mythical bungalow Long Hazard. My childhood
homes were owned by the Church of England or the patron of the parish or by God himself—does it matter? They
didn't belong to my parents, and they would never belong
to me. They were meagerly maintained by an institution
called the Queen Anne's Bounty, which was part of my
childhood folklore, like the Great Western Railway and
On His Majesty's Service. Queen Anne dealt with damp
courses, dry rot, and such major disasters as may happen to
large and ancient houses; but not bountifully. "We'll have
to ask Queen Anne" seemed a very normal remark to me,
though always ominous.

Apart from the furniture, the textures and colors and
smells, I remember very little about the inside of the vicarage; my feeling, which must of course be inaccurate, is that
I was seldom in it. The dining room was oak-paneled, the
dark passages covered in the ubiquitous Maggs matting and
lit with oil lamps; there was a small, steamy bathroom in
which, after my bath, I would be given a plate of gruel
called Frame Food. The kitchen had high windows and a
stone-flagged floor, and somewhere near it—the one place
inside the house that I can still almost touch—was the

Lamp Room. Here a lugubrious fellow named Tom—my
father's batman in the war, after which he became resident
handyman and purveyor of gloom—polished the oil lamps,
trimmed their wicks, puffed on their fragile glass funnels,
and refueled them. It seemed to be a full-time job, and one
of the few occasions I remember seeing Tom out of the
Lamp Room was the day when he poured a large can of
water over me in the kitchen passage. I don't remember
whether the water was hot or cold, but pour it, quite deliberately, he did. He was not a friendly man.

My natural infant squint didn't right itself; at the age of
three, I was made to wear glasses. I hated them, and with
doglike determination buried them again and again in the
rose bed, the sand pit, the compost heap. There were many
more final and destructive things I could have done with
them—dropped them in the water butt, burned them on
the bonfire, trampled them to death—but for some reason I
preferred burial, as less final and more ceremonious. I was
always asked (kindly, I think) where I had buried them,
and they were usually unearthed, though often they were
bent or cracked beyond repair. They soon bought me inde-
structible steel frames, which weighed down my nose and
were firmly latched behind my ears. I also had a large,
heavy instrument of medieval design which was meant to
exercise my wayward eyes. It consisted of two tubes attached to a kind of bridge: Into the end of one tube I
would slot a slide of, say, a bird; into the other, a slide
depicting a cage. With my eyes, and a certain amount of
manipulation of the binoculars, I then made the bird go
into the cage. There were many slides of this kind, dogs to

be put in kennels, sheep in fields, flowers into vases, and so on. It was a satisfactory game, though it appeared to have no effect at all on my eyes, which immediately swiveled back on their independent tracks, the left eager to catch what the right might miss.

It seems to me that most of my life was spent out of doors. I had a kingdom, or country, in the shrubbery behind the herbacious border: It was called Bath-hound, and was an excellent burial ground for the glasses, and for maggoty thrushes in shoe-box coffins. Another convenient thing about it was that all morality was reversed there: The fairies, elves, and pixies of my nursery mythology were evil beyond belief; ogres, witches, demons, dragons, and wicked stepmothers were radiantly good. I have no idea why it was called Bath-hound. But that was its name, and that was how I ordered it; or, as I would have preferred, disordered it.

Next to the vicarage was the Coles farm, separated from our garage and outhouses by no more than a narrow, flagged path—the gabled wing must have filled the discreet distance that once was between them. I thought the Coles family was closely related to God, though I knew He had never married, and therefore Farmer Coles might be a brother, or anyway some relative near enough to account for the close resemblance: A white, curly beard entirely covered his enormous chest, I never saw him without his round tweed hat, and his normal tone of voice was a roar that sent the chickens flying. Jim, the farmer's son, had a beaming face the color of weathered brick, and a bushy yel-

IN THE FIRST PLACE 63

low mustache. Mrs. Coles was spherical and rosy, with a center parting, a bun like a bun, and a rich chuckle. She had rather pale daughters, as such women tend to have. In their parlor there were tinkling prisms hanging from fragile glass stems on the mantelpiece; they shot rainbows around the dark room and made me feel strangely devout.

Perhaps it was my evil eye, careering wildly in the opposite direction to its twin, that caused Farmer Coles to call me "rum." "You're a rum gal!" he would thunder at me from his farmyard, seeing me perched high on a vicarage roof or wall. "You're a rum gal, all right!" When he was safely out of the way, I would climb down into the farmyard, which was more interesting than Bath-hound. Chickens laid eggs, cows were milked, pigs were slaughtered, cats ate mice, dogs ate rats, the horses pulled wagons, the rabbits became stew, the geese were for Christmas, and everything cultivated in the garden was edible. I raked the hay down through holes in the loft floor into the cows' and horses' mangers; I collected eggs, and carried milk in a slopping pail, though I never milked a cow, because I was scared of them. For the same reason, I rode a hay wagon but never a horse. There were long, timeless times when I did nothing, listening to the swish and thud of the cattle, becoming slack-mouthed and gormless from inhaling dung and hay and the sweet, icy air of the dairy.

My father's parish extended beyond Chilton to the village of Brill and the hamlet of Dorton, where my glamorous godmother, Jean Clemow, lived with a tall lady in an opera cloak and monocle, known as John. Jean was well known—even by me—to be in love with my father, whom she had met in Salonika during the war, while she was girlishly nursing the wounded. So great was her passion that she had bought a house in Dorton to be near him. John was presumably some sort of alibi. Later, and perhaps out of spite, John changed her name to Marie, making the whole thing more confusing. My mother appeared to take it all in her rapid, but ladylike stride. Jean, who always wore ruffles at her wrists and throat and the finest of silk stockings, took little interest in me; indeed, she probably found me repulsive. John, on the other hand, taught me about birds' nests. They were both, I think, wealthy.

I know that my father did not conduct services at Dorton every Sunday. The village was so small that even the obligatory two or three would have been hard—without Jean and John—to gather together more than a few times a year; the church was so small that even two or three made a crowd. However, my father sometimes took me with him to Dorton, perhaps as chaperon, but ostensibly to open the gates that protected the estate from the hoi polloi. I would ride the running board of the Morris, slithering off to unlatch the white gate, hold it open, shut it again. I was useful. I was very seldom useful, and I enjoyed it. Of my godmother's house I have, except for a faint sense of discomfort, no memory at all.

I imagine that most children brought up by clergymen list churches very high in their memories of places. To me, the church was an office, to which my father, reluctantly and with a great deal of fuss, went once a week. I was taught practically nothing of conventional Anglican religion, apart from its songs—in which, like those of Cole Porter, I was for many years word-perfect—and I was still too young for my father to transmit to me his bewildered dismay at the degeneration of God. My mother, as usual, kept her own counsel. Jean Clemow brought me a carved Virgin and Child from Oberammergau and my father had a very small crucifix—a relic of his ordination, perhaps—which hung inside a little Gothic box, with doors that opened and shut. In some curious way I confused this with his book on female anatomy—perhaps because he kept it in the same drawer in his desk, which was full of mysteries.

But on my weekday visits to the church with my mother, I became familiar with the dead and buried. There is an elaborate monument to a family called Croke in the chapel. Sir John and his wife, Elizabeth, who died around the beginning of the seventeenth century, lie stiff, with praying hands, their feet flexed, their noses pointed toward heaven. They lie on top of their tombs, and around it kneel the tiny figures of their eight sons and three daughters—symmetrical, devout, but entirely out of proportion to their huge, stern parents. The whole edifice is protected by iron railings. I would stare through the railings at the miniature but adult children (two, I believe, were judges) and then up to the knight and his lady who, whatever they were, were not at rest. I couldn't understand why their children were such midgets, or why they occupied such an inferior position, diminished down there as though they were in hell. I never told anyone how much this troubled me.

There was another memorial—a tablet on the wall, which must have been one of the first things I ever read, puzzling through the confusion of *f*'s and *s*'s:

Julia Francef Carter
youngeft daughter
of George Richard Carter
of Chilton Houfe Efq
and
Julia hif Wife
died November 2nd 1780 in her 14th year
and
if buried here in the Family vault

She waf a pattern to thofe of her age & promifed, had
her life been extended, to have been, af waf her beloved
Sifter Lady Aubrey, an ornament to her fex and an honor
to her ftation.

I was a little jealous of Julia Frances for being, potentially, so ornamental and honorable, being well aware, even in my felf-fatifaction, that I was neither.

2

The purpose of the Little People's Garden was to provide me with company, my brother being away and the Hubbards unsuitable, and to teach me basic skills like blanket stitch, adding up beads, Hymns A & M. I could already read, and boarding school was not considered necessary. I suppose my mother hoped to make a small financial profit, and perhaps she did. My impression is that she didn't spend quite so much time in the kitchen, and was more lively: Once, certainly, she took us for a walk and read *Tales of the Norsemen* aloud to us by a stream—perhaps we had a picnic, but the memorable thing is that she was alone with us in the outside world.

The children were recruited from families of soldiers or civil servants who were quelling or administering the British Empire. They seemed pale and overdressed, and may have been dreadfully homesick for a while. I know my mother must have been splendid with them, in an auntlike sort of way, but my egoism—or sense of security—was such that I now remember nothing about them except their pallor and their names, Jocelyn, Michael, Brian, Gwen . . . I know there was no favoritism. When one of us was frightened by a thunderstorm in the night, my mother provided toast and dripping for us all. I wasn't jealous, and didn't feel them to be usurpers. My Maggs mother had never seemed to love me particularly, so there was nothing to usurp—and my father had departed to the army hut.

In fact, it was all very enjoyable. The Little People's dormitory—previously my father's bedroom—had a row of five or six little oak beds with stenciled motifs on their little oak headboards; and the schoolroom—previously the drawing room—had five or six little folding tables, five or six extremely small chairs, and an enormous blackboard. It also had green baize notice boards, on which would be posted news of the seasons and reports on our nature studies, hips and haws, thistles and robins. Uncle Will's matting was smooth and shiny in the schoolroom, woven out of something like straw and less painful to bare feet than the rough coconut. There was a big, chintz-covered armchair, the doll's house, and a toy chest built all around the window bay. So miniature were the People in my mother's Garden that a photograph shows my brother, around the age of ten, kneeling at one of the tables much as Gulliver could have knelt, towering, over some Lilliputian desk. I believe that this unappealing picture was intended for a prospectus or brochure, and I believe that the prospectus was home-made, in a photograph album with thick black pages, the captions written in some sort of white ink. In the same photograph, I am sitting at another table, looking absurdly studious, wearing a linen sailor dress, and boots to support my supposedly weak ankles. We both appear deformed, and I am surprised that the Little People's parents gave us another thought.

Obviously, my mother had to import a governess to teach us spelling and hymns and how to grow beans on blotting paper. I remember only one, Miss Meredith; she was about nineteen, and did her hair in loose earphones skewered with tortoise-shell pins. I don't even know whether she was pretty.

My mother must have realized that it would be hazard-ous to have a young woman about the place. But since at no time in my life did I ever know my parents to share a bedroom, let alone a bed, she may have thought of Miss Meredith as a red rag to lure the bull away (and eventually destroy him?); she could stay safe behind her fence of ap-pearances. Certainly there seems no good reason why she should engage a nineteen-year-old girl rather than some re-tired, botany-minded spinster, who would have been more to her taste. In any case, and inevitably, my father fell passionately in love. Since he was living in the army hut and communicating, I think, only by notes, we were not aware of the drama. We were not even aware that he actually went away with Miss Meredith for an entire week—it must have been the holidays, and possibly only from Monday to Saturday, since he still had a job to do. I knew that he sometimes drove to London for the day, but not that my mother went along as apparent chaperon, perched in the back of the Morris Oxford while Miss Meredith sat beside my father; they would drop her at some convenient spot, like Selfridges, and pick her up again in the evening (who looked after us meanwhile? I don't know), and appearances were held high. When the affair ended, and Miss Meredith left, my father returned to the house, though I don't know where he slept. He kept well away from us, spending much of his time digging or mowing or building, great physical efforts which, he said, got the sugar going in his blood. The only indication of my mother's feelings about the whole business was that throughout her life she referred to the girl as "Meredith," without any prefix, as though she had been a man.

I connect Meredith with my father, and don't remember very much she taught and nothing she said. Perhaps there were other governesses, before or after, and they all proba- bly came through an organization called the Parents' Na- tional Educational Union, known as the PNEU—I thought it was a shipping line until I realized that its purpose was to provide instruction in the home for children too delicate or retarded or privileged to leave it. We sang "Oh Worship

the King, All-glorious Above" and were made to eat grated
carrot and were taken for invigorating walks. Most of the
Little People stayed the year round, and the devastated
postman brought letters from Ceylon, Bombay, Nigeria,
and Hong Kong; there were exotic gifts, too—lengths of
shantung, ivory elephants, a lacquered sewing box for my
mother, quinquereme of Ninevah. We learned the verses
of Robert Louis Stevenson:

> *Little Indian, Sioux or Crow,*
> *Little frosty Eskimo,*
> *Little Turk or Japanee,*
> *Oh! Don't you wish that you were me?*
>
> *You have seen the scarlet trees*
> *And the lions overseas;*
> *You have eaten ostrich eggs,*
> *And turned the turtles off their legs.*
>
> *Such a life is very fine,*
> *But it's not as nice as mine:*
> *You must often, as you trod,*
> *Have wearied not to be abroad.*

Safe in the Home Counties, we were encouraged to
paint the strange landscapes that I had never seen—small
pyramids and huge camels and biblical palm trees, pin-
gollywogs in deserts. On Empire Day, which also happened
to be my father's birthday, the village blossomed with
Union Jacks and my father hauled up the flag on the
church tower.

Apart from this gentle jingoism—much of which must
have been for the comfort of the Little People—we were
entirely undisturbed by the outside world. Probably my father read *The Times* over in his hut, and listened to his

wireless set, which had an octagonal loudspeaker hung high on the wall, and of which he was very proud. He told us that he had once been mistaken for Stanley Baldwin, and perhaps it was this gratifying resemblance that made him, at this time, a fervent Conservative. All I knew of the Gen-- eral Strike was that my father became something impressive called a "special constable" and went off in the Morris Oxford with a tin hat and a truncheon on a leather thong— he was always grateful for action, however unsound the principles. Nobody told us that he was armed against communist revolutionaries; but nobody told us, either, that a face worker in the pit was earning a maximum of ninety shillings a week. My mother's social conscience, so lively in the Redstocks days, must have been dampened by trying to keep up appearances on little more than a miner's wage. We probably made a number of cowslip balls during the General Strike, and picked many handfuls of primroses— the truncheon ended up in our dressing-up box.

An important part of our middle-class Englishness was the seaside holiday—no baking on a Mediterranean beach, but lungfuls of Atlantic ozone, gales, hard sand, buckets and spades, shrimping nets, plimsolls baked by the salt sun. We were taken to Sheringham, on the Norfolk coast, and to Seaview, near Ventnor, on the Isle of Wight. The journeys, particularly to Seaview, must have been ecstatically exciting, but I remember little about them except the hot, dusty smell of our compartment on the train (third class, I'm sure), the buttons on the uncomfortable upholstery, the photographs of scenic views on either side of the tarnished mirror, the *duddledada* of the wheels on the track, the banshee howl as we entered a tunnel, the lovely dirt—smut, even grit, in our eyes, grimy faces, blackened hands. In the lavatories there was a sign which said, "Passengers will please refrain from passing water when the train is standing in a station or a siding"—poetry. We climbed on the overhead luggage racks and turned the heating from Off to Cold to Hot and back again and longed to pull the Communication Cord, but the penalty was five pounds and beyond our means. The driver and fireman—wearing a sack on his head to protect him from the heat and flying cinders—were in blackface and their teeth shone; they would talk to you, if you felt like making conversation before the train started. My mother always closed the windows before we went into a tunnel, and red-hot sparks flew by, sometimes a whole sheet of flame. When the train stopped, it gave a huge, exhausted sigh and then there was extraordinary silence, like no other silence in the world.

> *The steam hissed. Someone cleared his throat,*
> *No one left and no one came*
> *On the bare platform . . .*

When, a few years later, I read Edward Thomas' "Adlestrop," I realized that the most important thing about reading is recognition—yes, yes, that's exactly how it was.

Then there was the first moment when we saw the sea, standing on the seats, clamoring at the windows for sight of that thin bright strip on the horizon; the first evening when, however tired we were, we were let loose on the beach, rediscovering last year's rock pool, digging for treasure buried long ago, when we were only six or seven. In the

Isle of Wight there was treacherous blue clay into which, we believed, you could sink and be smothered. I thought of the girl in the Hans Andersen story who used a loaf of bread as a stepping stone over a bog, and sank down and down among vile reptiles, punishment for selfishness and ingratitude. My mother constantly told me that I was selfish and ungrateful. But on one of these holidays, while I was busy perfecting a sand castle before the tide came and swept it away, I heard her say something that might have been interpreted as praise: "One thing to be said for Peggy," she observed to whoever was sitting in the next deck chair, "she does have determination."

My father never came to the seaside, unless it was Deal, which didn't count. One summer we had a guardian—nanny or governess, I don't know—called Miss Crow, who wore black stockings with her bathing suit. I only know my brother came with us, at least occasionally, because of a picture of a blurred boy on the beach at Sheringham, with myself in rubber waders that cut into the tops of my legs and were always wet and gritty with sand (but what was he feeling?); and another of a smiling boy holding a shrimping net and sitting on the edge of a rowboat, while I intently examine some shell or dead crab and take no notice.

Such voyages only happened once a year. From September until July, our expeditions were far more modest. The nearest town to Chilton was Thame, its wide main street crowded on market day, seedsmen's shops and saddlers, ironmongers, bakers (the smell of fresh bread—my mother would never allow us to eat it until it was a day old, and soon turned against white bread altogether, telling us that it was polluted with china clay from Cornwall), the pharmacist's window with beautiful carboys of green and red and blue water, inside, in the half dark, remedies for chilblains and croup. There was a fair once a year—roundabouts and slides, coconut shies and toffee apples, but we never saw it at night—and I remember the extraordinary, flickering image of Jackie Coogan thrown onto a collapsible screen in some church hall, barn, or misappropriated chapel.

In Thame a dramatic gentleman called John Fothergill kept a famous pub, the Spread Eagle. It was famous because of its owner, who wore velvet jackets and buckled shoes, and was reputed to be a close friend of Augustus John and other distant luminaries. For a short while some of us attended a dancing class there. Perhaps we lolloped around being elves, rabbits, frogs, and blossoming tulips; or maybe Mr. Fothergill, with his artistic connections, inclined toward Isadora Duncan, and we staggered about trying to express woe, radiance, and social conscience. Dancing at home was (like everything else) more enjoyable, and we frequently performed impromptu ballets, and dramas of inordinate length and, I'm sure, tedium. My mother was a good audience, because she provided cake and lemonade, though I'm sure she wished I wouldn't show off quite so much.

We were occasionally taken to Oxford—a journey of about fifteen miles, and therefore an expedition. I think that once or twice we were left to play in the gardens of St. John's College while my mother went shopping; I think the gardens were very dull. But coming down the steep hill from Headington there was—and still is—a delicate footbridge, apparently leading from treetop to treetop, slung across the dark ravine of the road. I looked forward to that, and to driving out into the light at the bottom of the hill, the sober tower of Magdalen (frivolous on May Day with boys' voices in summer carols) and the flat green river, the jostling High, the Corn, and the Broad (my father was always very careful to use Oxonian terms for these places—he also called breakfast "brekker," which somehow embarrassed me). There was a very dignified shop called Elliston and Cavell, where money and receipts whizzed in lead containers along wires from the counter to the cashier and back again, and there were high chairs for the customers to sit on while they chose their elastic or hosiery. Elliston and Cavell had all the hauteur and stuffiness that I would soon associate with Marshall and Snelgrove, Dickins and Jones, Debenham and Freebody, emporiums where all the ladies seemed to look vaguely like Virginia Woolf and were perhaps wracked with the same genteel passions.

Apart from these voyages, we stayed at home. For eight years I waddled or trotted, scurried or scuffed around the garden, the orchard, the farmyard, sometimes in the company of the Little People, sometimes not. And then came the day when a Mr. Ravenscroft, fat, red-faced, dressed in a black suit, black hat, and sanctimonious smile, was introduced to me—in the orchard, for some reason—as the new Vicar of Chilton. We were moving, it seemed immediately, to Thornton Heath, a suburb of London.

It was, I think, early September, the apples not yet ripe, the leaves rusting. "We are moving to London and this is Mr. Ravenscroft, who will be coming to live here," they

said, or something like that. And Mr. Ravenscroft smiled
and smiled, barely creasing his tight red skin, little black
shoes stamped firmly in my grass, black hat set perfectly
straight on his loathsome head. Nobody had asked my permission. Nobody explained why. I hated Mr. Ravenscroft,
new incumbent of my territory, invader of Bath-hound,
and I hate him still, in whatever prim Anglican heaven he
now illegitimately resides.

In the Second Place

1

It isn't too fanciful to say that something came to an end that day in the orchard: And my impression is that what set was some kind of perpetual, clement, domestic, and endearing sun. The light changed. Though people—my parents—remained constant for a while, we lived in a different place and climate. In order to survive we had to alter, or to use parts of ourselves that had so far gone unexercised. This was not to the good. Therefore it is in a way accurate to say that Mr. Ravenscroft, however unwittingly, destroyed some kind of innocence.

Thornton Heath is attached to London by a sprawling network of suburbs, most of them within the County of London boundaries, but so far removed from the city I would know in later years that they still seem to me, with my provincial background, foreign. "Our" electric railway line, its destination Victoria, clattered from Clapham Junction, past the end of our garden, to Streatham and Wandsworth Common; and by bus one could range from Mitchum to Penge, south Croydon, Purley and Coulsdon, north to Balham and Tooting and Lewisham. That these terrible places were home to millions of people, that children found mysteries in their patches of garden or would remember their neighborhood streets and shops with pleasure, never occurred to me. For the first few months the place was—anyway to my mother and me—unrelievedly hellish.

The vicarage, 1, Norbury Avenue, Thornton Heath, near Croydon, Surrey—it even had a telephone, which surely must have caused some excitement ("This is the vicar's daughter," I would say when I gingerly answered it, and never understood why that caused so much indulgent laughter, since it was true). I clearly remember my first sight of the house from a taxi, my horrified disbelief. Gabled and stuccoed, identical with all the other houses on that side of the road. I simply couldn't imagine *people* crammed at such close quarters, walking inches instead of yards, yards instead of miles, surely eating celluloid food off tin plates no bigger than a farthing, climbing into match-stick beds at night. I trudged reluctantly down the long, thin patch of garden, bordered on each side with dilapidated, creosoted fences; at the bottom of it there was a rough patch with a broken-down hut, and a few old sauce-pans rusting in what I supposed was London grass; then there was another, wire fence and the railway line. The electrc trains went very fast, and shot blue flashes from their wheels; they didn't seem to have drivers.

My mother, though she didn't say so to me at the time, was heartbroken. She must have had the walls distempered, and hung up her linen curtains, and moved in her lovely furniture, in numb misery. Only one of the Little People—Michael?—came with us, but there was some sort of alter-cation with his mother (perhaps mine was too possessive) and he left. The surly Tom came with us, too, but it was not the sort of life to which he was accustomed. He came into the kitchen brandishing a few sprigs of wilted and polluted parsley, gave in his notice, and went off to become somebody's butler. My mother had no friends in London, and no prospect of any in Thornton Heath.

My father, however, had a new lease of life. He started a Youth Club and preached his splendid, meaningless sermons to huge congregations of children—fifteen-year-old girls, who adored him, and spotty, adolescent boys. "Life!" he bellowed. "Believe in Life!" He grasped the edge of the pulpit, tears ran down his face, he laughed, he flung his spectacles into the congregation, narrowly missing my mother and myself, who sat, suffering tortures of embarrassment and misery, in the front pew. He was asked to preach the Armistice Day sermon at Aldershot, in front of King George V—I don't know whether my mother went to this ceremony, and I certainly didn't, but it was said that my father's pulpit oratory made the King weep into his handkerchief, which may or may not be true. In any case, he must have felt that, in spite of the hollow where his beliefs used to be, he might still be a success if he toed the line and didn't kick against the pricks or beat his head against a brick wall—phrases of my mother's with which he and I were very familiar.

I was eight, and my education was to be designed, whenever possible, to mirror his current ideas. Since these were now conformist, I was dressed in a small gym slip, white flannel blouse, and tie, and sent to the junior department of Croydon High School. I remember nothing about it except standing to attention behind a desk, wearing my scratchy uniform and holding my breath against the smell of disinfectant. Fortunately for us all, my father discovered anthroposophy.

I am still not absolutely sure what anthroposophy is, beyond being a form of theosophy invented by a Dr. Rudolf Steiner in Germany after World War I. As my father, on his conversion or illumination, immediately sent me to an anthroposophist school in Streatham, I should perhaps know more. But if I set myself to find out, it would destroy a certain mystery and glamour. I prefer to leave it as it was, something which, however briefly and tenuously, brought my parents together.

They were both inclined toward theosophy, spiritualism, anything that would add interest to a life spent cutting up cubes of bread for Communion, or carrying cans of water from the kitchen tap to the front, or footing the bill for sacramental wine. For once, thanks to Dr. Steiner, they were in agreement. My father may have read a few books, but my mother made copious notes as well: "The physical body developed thro' former evolutions of the earth. The germ of physical body was laid in the Old Saturn, the etheric body during the Old Sun & the astral body in Old Moon periods. . . . In sleep the Ego and Astral body leave the physical as far as the nerve and blood systems are concerned, & enter the spiritual world whence they send down forces into our bodily organs. All important that selfless and fearless thoughts are in the mind when entering sleep. Materialistic thoughts cultivate bacilli, as they call forth Lucerific forces. . . ."

This was the time when she became very intimate with

the dead, and frequently told me that I should always be
civil to any ghosts I might meet about the place. This
scared me. She even met ghosts in the vicarage, Thornton
Heath, which couldn't have been much more than twenty
years old. I don't think her father, or brothers and sisters,
ever visited her there; but she would report having long
conversations with old ladies who came and sat by her bed.
According to her notes, the dead are very vulnerable, and
need continuous nourishment from our spiritual thoughts.
If all they get is a diet of materialism and egoism, they
starve (but not, of course, to death). It is kind to read to
them, since this enhances their consciousness, but very
harmful indeed to wish they were still alive, because this
shakes their confidence. It wasn't exactly gloomy—the dead
were quite cheerful, provided they were kept incessantly
entertained and stimulated—but it did add to the responsibilities of life. Now it seemed that I was letting down
ghosts, as well as people, by being selfish and ungrateful. I
didn't want to read to them, or take them for walks. I
wanted them to keep quiet and go away. I was therefore
being rude to my mother's friends, and that would make
her sad.

My father, who needed something a little more active
than old ladies sitting by his bed, went to a few séances and
swore by Sir Oliver Lodge. I saw photographs of astral bodies coming or going, of protoplasm streaming out of people's heads. It may all have been very necessary and comforting to my parents, brought up in the stern materialist
ethic of nineteenth-century Wesleyanism, but to me it was
simply spooky. It was a relief to be told that Dr. Steiner

had a practical side: His concern for the astral body was so great, it seemed, that he had submitted a design for a new sleeping car, suited to astral needs, to the officials of the German Railway: he had also invented a bicycle that was powered by an up-and-down, rather than circular, motion of the legs, since astral legs simply hate going round and round. I don't wish to be flippant about mysticism, and I suppose it is possible that Dr. Steiner was a true mystic. His bulging glare—very similar to that of Hitler—from the photographs in every room of the New School certainly made me uncomfortable every time I glanced at it. His physical body, anyway, had died some years previously, from eating poisoned cakes. His other ones presumably flitted off to Jupiter, where all anthroposophist souls stop for a while on their way to Venus, or so my mother apparently believed. I felt I had slim chance of joining any Higher Hierarchy on earth, let alone on some remote planet.

However, there was very little of this at the New School —anyway, nothing that I could actually see. It was, as I remember it, a satisfactorily big red brick house in a leafy road off Streatham Common, with a large garden, real trees, and stone steps leading up to a dignified terrace. I wore my own clothes for a few days, while they diagnosed my temperament. The prognosis was red, for choleric. So I wore red smocks in the summer, and red jerseys in the winter, and went to school on a Number 58 bus—some of them were still open on top, and it was a thoroughly pleasant experience to sit up there sucking a gobstopper, taking it out now and then to see how its color had changed, watching the world go by down below. Sometimes I was allowed to bicycle, and then I would hang on to the back of the 58 bus and let it tow me. The derring-do that had sent me shinning up walls and trees and over rooftops at Chilton had very little outlet in Thornton Heath, and my opportunities for showing off were limited. I remember crying as though it were a new achievement, and having tempers and fits of passion. But, as a family, we seemed for a while almost normal.

People sometimes came in the evenings, when I was in bed, and they seemed to be having conversations. My parents and I even went for a walk together on Mitchum Common one Good Friday, my father probably dying for air after a lengthy service and worried about the Easter Offering. He took me to the Davis Theatre, Croydon, to a special showing for the clergy of *The King of Kings*. The bishop's children were kneeling in prayer on the red-carpeted staircase, and my father was so disgusted by the whole thing that he bustled me out before the Crucifixion. Once, when we were in Deal for our summer holidays, he put his arm around my mother as they walked up the road, and she didn't move away.

But I did. One day I was sent to his bedroom with a message—he must have been ill, for I never saw my father in bed before, and never after, until he was dying—and he asked me to get into bed with him, which I did reluctantly, being fully clothed and not sleepy. He then asked if he could put his little finger into me, and held it up, presumably to show how small it was. I doubt whether I dared to say no, but somehow avoided the curious game and es-

caped. It was the beginning of many years of difficulty and
discomfort, seldom bursting into outrage, which convinced
me, in the end, that I hated him: which I didn't.

What I hated most, from that day on, was his shame.
My poor father (whom I did not then think poor) had no
style; he was all fingers and thumbs, slobbering and puffing
and desperate with guilt. I dreaded being left alone with
him. I was a demonstrative child (his daughter), and it
was chilly not to be able to throw my arms around him and
climb about on him and give him a great hug, as I often
wanted to do. My mother's abhorrence of sex made it impossible for her to talk to me, and impossible to talk to. Beginning with the book on female anatomy, my father told
me (again and again) what facts of life he knew; but my
mother told me nothing. As far as I could tell, she had no
physical life at all, beyond eating and sleeping and hurrying
and sometimes getting mysteriously ill. Perhaps one of the
reasons why she was so fond of the dead was that they were
sexless.

My father was very much a man of his time and place.
He had lost his faith, but none of the new ideas he desperately tried to put in the vacuum would fit. They were made
for psychologists, philosophers, academics, people with
large brains and narrow hearts. He was constantly being
told that sex was a great and glorious experience that could
even be enjoyed by middle-class ladies; but he was a clergyman with a frigid wife, so how could he find out? It must
have been like a continual party going on next door, the
Russells and the Lawrences and the Huxleys arriving with
their merry, liberated cries, Havelock Ellis for charades and

Sigmund Freud for breakfast. But there he sat, in 1, Norbury Avenue, Thornton Heath, without the guts to gatecrash, without the humility to listen if he had; boiling with frustration and envy, without a soul to talk to, let alone anyone to twine garlands around his unmentionable manhood. I am not surprised that he couldn't keep his hands off his daughter; and I sincerely believe that he suffered more than I did. I at least had a future; he didn't even have a past.

Anyway, it was best dealt with by not dealing with it at all. At the New School, I recited my personal maxim, chosen particularly for me, each morning: "Venture Valiantly Towards the Goal You Have Set Before You." I did anthroposophist exercises for my squint, painted very messy pictures on wet paper, sat on top of an American boy named Eric and banged his head very deliberately on the asphalt tennis court. I had a friend called Wilmay Ward, whose family was in some way vaguely exotic, and I fell passionately in love with my music teacher, "Muki" Kaufmann.

2

Dr. Kaufmann was at least thirty. He had the most beautiful, slender calves below his elegant plus-fours. I think he had been sent from Poland, with a label around his neck, when he was a child. He had a brown, thin, gentle face and light brown hair streaked blond by the sun. He taught me to play the recorder, and I worshiped him.

I sat on his knee on the terrace; his brown hand touched my bare thigh, and he smiled and said, "You're always warm." I covered my face with blackboard chalk and fell down in a stage faint on the tennis court to get his attention. Very occasionally, he came to supper at the vicarage; the excitement of him coming upstairs to say good night to me was almost more than I could bear. I wanted to hug him forever and never let him go.

My mother sometimes took me on the bus to a place called Riddlesdown, which approximated, less rather than more, to the country. There was an open space, and a steep hill rising to a cluster of trees. The hill was covered in thistles. I would take off my sandals and tell myself that "Muki" Kaufmann was in mortal danger, imprisoned in the forest, and the only thing that would save him was if someone loved him enough to climb the hill barefoot. It was exquisite agony, and I was oddly philosophical about not finding Dr. Kaufmann when I got to the top.

Being in love and avoiding ghosts took up much of my time. I was writing sickly little verses modeled on "Flower Fairies of the Spring/Summer/Autumn" and descriptive pieces of appalling banality about the countryside. "I am a tramp," I wrote, in orange ink with a broad Relief nib, "that is all the introduction I need just to tell you that I am—a tramp. Who's life can be better than mine, tramping, tramping, tramping, always by the road side, a long, white dusty road that seems to stretch on and on until the worlds end, calling you to seek your adventure on it! Some people think it is better to wash themselves in beautiful baths with hot water and servants to wait on them: not so the tramp . . ." and so on, tramp, tramp, tramp, tramp,

deafening in its lack of talent. However, I must have had
ambition of a sort, and when my father managed to get a
story of mine printed in *The Review of Reviews* (I imagine he paid), I was immensely proud, except for the fact
that they printed it with all the spelling mistakes, which I
thought they might have corrected.

I had already read *Black Beauty, Owd Bob, The Children of the New Forest, The Secret Garden,* and, of
course, *Lorna Doone.* At Thornton Heath I became ad-
dicted to Jeffery Farnol and, to a lesser extent, the
Baronness Orczy. I was embarrassed by my father's render-
ing of Browning, but loved his Alfred Noyes:

> *Tlot-tlot in the frosty silence! Tlot-tlot in the*
> > *echoing night!*
> *Nearer he came and nearer! Her face was like a light!*
> *Her eyes grew wide for a moment; she drew one last deep*
> > *breath,*
> *Then her fingers moved in the moonlight,*
> > *Her musket shattered the moonlight,*
> *Shattered her breast in the moonlight, and warned him—*
> > *with her death.*
>
> *Back he spurred like a madman, shrieking a curse to the*
> > *sky,*
> *With the white road smoking behind him and his rapier*
> > *brandished high!*
> *Blood-red were his spurs i' the golden noon; wine-red*
> > *was his velvet coat,*
> *When they shot him down on the highway,*
> > *Down like a dog on the highway,*
> *And he lay in his blood on the highway, with the bunch of*
> > *lace at his throat.*

To this braggadocio—I particularly admired the mad-
man, the rapier, the blood-red spurs—I added the mocca-
sins and feathered headdress of Hiawatha, who, when my

mother took me to see the musical version at the Albert Hall, became my greatest hero after Dr. Kaufmann. She made me a Hiawatha costume and my father made a bow and arrows; I tracked red deer by the railway line and sat cross-legged in a wigwam painted (by my brother? I wonder) with sacred emblems. It wasn't a very suitable role for Thornton Heath, but it gave me enormous pleasure.

My father had a sonorous tenor voice, and now that I could pick out a tune on the piano, he began to sing for me —"Because," "The Gentle Maiden," "The Slender Boy," "Scots What Hae," Wagner's "Abendstern"—he was very moved by Wagner. I rather liked him when he was singing; he made a good, rich sound. For myself, I preferred popular songs bought on small, sixpenny records from Woolworth's. I played them on a red portable Gramophone— "Tiptoe Through the Tulips," "All by Yourself in the Moonlight," "The Wedding of the Painted Doll," hits from *The Desert Song* and *Bittersweet*. Both my parents had a violent, puritanical prejudice against what they called jazz, so I would stuff my socks into the loudspeaker in the hope that they wouldn't hear it and be angry. My father bought a 16-mm cinema projector for his Youth Club, and when my mother was ill he brought it over and we saw *Felix the Cat*, *The Inkspots*, and Charlie Chaplin. I also was allowed to go to the cinema, once, with my friend Doreen Everett. She was older than I—possibly as old as my brother—and sometimes wore lipstick. We saw a film about the sinking of the *Titanic*, in which Tom Walls and Ralph Lynn played a pair of drunkards. I couldn't understand this, never having seen anyone drunk, but found the icebergs very convincing and was much moved when everybody sang "Nearer My God to Thee." I was not allowed to go and see *The Student Prince*, a fact that provoked one of my increasingly frequent furies, lying on the drawing room floor behind the sofa and bellowing as though, for the third time that week, the world had come to an end.

Because Thornton Heath was so horrible, and most of the diversions (even the friendly dead) unsatisfactory, I spent most of the school holidays away from home: Either I would go with my mother to Bowerhill, or, in the summer, my father took temporary jobs in the country; occasionally, as a last resort, I was sent to stay with my grandmother Nellie at Silex, The Grove, Deal, Kent. It was there, with my father's eldest brother, my Uncle Bertie, that I spent one of the most memorable days of my life.

My Uncle Bertie was the only member of my two families who, on my own rating, had achieved real eminence. He was fifty at that time—a year younger than my mother—and had seen quite another aspect of that turnabout half century.

While my father, as a boy, was perpetually being "converted," "convinced of sin," and other such sentimentalities, Bertie had become a heretic at the age of five, after discovering that he could make a rainbow by squirting the garden hose in the sunlight, and immediately proclaiming his own divinity. He was beaten for this, but not cowed. At the three schools he and my father had attended together, Bertie excelled academically, while my father was

dismissed as a dunce. The fact that Bertie was expelled
from Queen's College, Taunton, for flagrant burglary, may
have been some comfort.

He became a medical student at Barts, but when my
grandfather died—which must, in fact, have been something of a financial relief—Bertie decided to go to work. He
took up "bum brushing"—a startling contemporary term
for "ushering," which in itself was a contemporary term for
teaching small boys the basics of Latin, algebra, and trig-
onometry. My father, though he may not have known it,
hated Bertie all his life. After that summer day, when I was
nine years old, I loved him.

Where my father was heavy and blunt, Bertie was sharp,
clever, with a waspish wit; where my father was constantly
on the sexual boil—however firmly the lid was kept down—
Bertie had a disdain, on the whole, for women; where my
father was constantly writing, to no avail, Bertie had published at least four books. In 1910 my father had got married, and settled down to a life of chronic agitation; that
same year, Bertie left for South America and twelve years
of legitimate piracy around the Pacific Ocean. About the
time my father was building his unsuccessful bungalow in
Buckinghamshire, Bertie sailed from Santiago for the
South Seas.

By 1914 he was running a copra plantation near Mos-
quito Bay in the New Hebrides. There, happily removed
from what he called "the Great Killing," he lived a peculiar and idyllic life, Beardsley's drawings for Salome on the
walls of his hut, duck and wild honey for dinner. He wrote
constant letters to his friend Bohun Lynch, published by

Constable in 1923 under the pseudonym "Asterisk" and the disarming title *Isles of Illusion*. I had not been allowed to read this remarkable book: "Though nothing will be found here to titillate the salacious," Bohun Lynch had written in his introduction, "the book is not recommended for the nursery shelf." And anyway, even in my childhood, there was still an air of disgrace around Uncle Bertie; for he had not only betrayed his country, keeping his distance in its time of need, but he had betrayed an entire ethic (and, perhaps, himself) by having a liaison with a native woman, siring a number of indeterminately colored children, and by making the whole unsavory business public, so that my grandmother could never hold up her head in Deal again. Perverse of me, perhaps, but these unknown cousins—I always imagined them beautiful, hibiscus in their hair, noble and lithe and the color of sandalwood— became my favorite contemporary relatives. They never heard of me, or Deal, or their grandmother, who was feared by God. Uncle Bertie abandoned them with very few pangs of conscience.

He had returned home to find himself erased from the family Bible. He probably knew, being a cynic, that this would be only a temporary disowning; nearly all the children had been crossed out and readmitted so often that the record pages looked like a shopping list made out by someone in a state of shock. Besides, he briefly found himself something of a literary lion. *Isles of Illusion* had been given two columns in *The Times*, an entire page in *The Times Literary Supplement*, fulsome praise from many American dailies and periodicals, and was the subject of a long article

by Sir John (then plain Jack) Squire. The book went into
many editions, in both England and America, and was
widely translated in Europe. Bertie, sticking all his press
cuttings into two very large albums, did not worry too
much about the Bible.

He had already written two successful thrillers, and
now began another book about the South Seas. This, too,
was published by Constable, but Bertie was ashamed of it.
Later, he wrote a novel of which he was really proud: It
was about life in a native brothel in Nouméa, capital of
New Caledonia, and the story was based on the winning by
a little Kanaka tart of *le gros lot* in the French National
Lottery. Michael Sadleir, of Constable, turned it down
with great reluctance. It was, he said, obscene.

During my early childhood, Bertie had returned to
ushering. He had occasionally been to stay with us at Chilton, but I was too concerned with my own life to notice
him very much. Then came the visit to Deal, and an invita-
tion to spend the day with him on his rabbit farm. This
was a new venture for him: Angora rabbits, the fashion at
that time being tickling Angora jumpers in pastel colors,
and horrid little hot hats and fluffy mittens and bed jackets
and anything that could be made out of that sickly and uncomfortable wool.

My uncle had revolutionary ideas about the upbringing
and education of children, by whom he meant boys. His attitude toward girls—insofar as he had one—was outrageous.
He, in fact, was outrageous. On June 17, 1918, he had written to Bohun Lynch, describing his "concubine's" labor:

So there I was with a Handbook of Obstetrics, howling directions to Topsy in Biche-la-mar, cursing the attendant midwives who wanted to kill the child, and generally enjoying myself. I fancy that I am in for another merry job about January 31st. I simply can't kick the poor little girl out for her "trouble." She places such implicit trust in me that it would be blackguardly to forsake her. If it were an ordinary sized native brat that she had to bear, things would doubtless pass off in the native fashion—work till sunset, bear the child at night, and up again next morning. But my colts—judging from Bilbil—are past all bearing. I hope, though, that this one will be a filly. Then Topsy shall have it all to her little self, which she longs for. Bilbil, of course, is my child, not Topsy's. Topsy is quite resigned. "Fashion b'long me feller, papa 'e look out picaninny where 'e man, piccaninny where 'e woman 'e b'long mama."

I hadn't, of course, read this. I didn't know that, in Uncle Bertie's terminology, I was a filly. Nevertheless, he took me over, if only to spite that overemotional, uneducated oaf I had for a father. He gave me a taste of freedom; possibly, even, a taste for it.

Oddly enough, there was a woman involved. I remember nothing about her except her name: Diane. It was an improbable name in connection with Bertie, particularly in the wilds of Kent. However, Diane was there; or her name was there. I was told to do whatever I liked. After puzzling for a short while—the possibilities seemed endless—I stripped off all my clothes and made a kind of cowboy costume out of the long grass. My appearance, topped with the steel rims, must have been eccentric, but possibly it reminded Bertie of the South Seas. In any case, I remained

in this costume all day, replenishing it as it disintegrated
until boredom with the design overcame modesty, and I
played around naked except for odd wisps of grass that
clung to me as though I were a small rake.

There was meat of some kind for lunch. I was told I
could eat it with my fingers, though I'm sure that neither
Bertie nor Diane said that fingers were made before forks—
an expression used by my female relatives to explain,
though not condone, my terrible table manners. It was my
Hiawatha period, and I pretended that I was gnawing
venison—hair, skin, and meat shining with oil and gravy.
Uncle Bertie approved. He then made his one mistake and
gave me a young rabbit, a nasty little thing with pink skin
under its long white hair, which for some reason I named
Galahad.

I shall never forget that day. If I had chosen to spend it
reading an unworthy book, or writing multiplication tables,
or doing nothing at all, I would have been equally acceptable. Nobody expected me to "join in," but nobody made
me feel an outcast, either. I didn't expect it to be repeated.
I was right—it never was.

My father's "locums" were a bit of a gamble, but they
usually turned out well. I remember vividly the excitement
of arriving at those strange vicarages, rectories, or even
deaneries, all of them splendid in comparison with the dismal, urban house we had left behind. One of the first
things to do—though strictly under my mother's super-
vision—was to strip all the rooms of their religious bric-a-
brac, palm crosses, photographs of dead bishops and live

curates, and put each roomful of junk into its own, labeled
cardboard box. Then my father started moving the furniture and my mother brought in flowers, wild if necessary.
She unpacked her tattered cookbook and put on her apron.
On Sundays my father startled a congregation of strangers,
and my mother cut the dead heads off somebody else's roses.

The deanery, Southampton, must have been something
of a mistake, because it was another city; and also my
brother was certainly present. But it was, for me at any
rate, a success. We woke on the first morning to find a traveling circus camped at the bottom of the garden, an ele-
phant chumping the hedge, a chimpanzee, hand in hand
with its owner, walking to the water tap. After that, for
two shillings each we sped to the Isle of Wight and back in
a speedboat called *Zip*. My father took us rowing on the
Solent, but the tide went out and we were stranded in miles
of mud; my father lost his temper and called my brother
"an insolent young pup." Young people (not children)
from Thornton Heath were there—girls with lipstick
(Doreen Everett among them) and tall boys in blue suits.
My hair was clenched back with a huge tortoise-shell barrette, which had an extraordinarily intricate mechanism of
springs and levers to keep it in place. I don't know whether
the young people were staying with us, or whether they
were independently in Southampton—but I do remember
the deck of a ferry boat where, by some miraculous feat of
clumsiness, I managed to introduce the sharp edge of this
barrette into the eye of one of the tall boys, who was called
Basil.

In Southampton, following the tradition of Bath-hound,

I staked my territory in a room or small loft above a garage or stable. I furnished it with an oak table found somewhere, and a jam jar full of marigolds. Tutored by my mother, but adding my own boundless Fletcher sentimentality, my tastes were not exactly insipid, but they were definitely sweet. Sweetness infected me for years—low beams, lattice windows, roses around the door, a kettle singing on the hearth, a pixie or two. I believed that colors, even of flowers, could "clash" (a poppy never grew next to a mauve peony in my mother's herbacious border), and that all innovations were, prima facie, "ugly." Picasso had been painting for three decades, but if my parents had ever heard of him they kept quiet about it; the most avant-garde drawings on their walls were scribbled by a lady of their acquaintance while in a state of trance.

The two most memorable pictures of my childhood were a Doré engraving of Satan being cast into hell, and a picture in the Bible of Solomon ordering the baby to be cut in half—the baby dangling by one foot, the soldier's scimitar at the ready. This upset me—or disturbed my fantasies—a great deal. It was removed from the Bible, which then lost all interest for me.

The Doré engraving was in a huge volume of *Paradise Lost*, which I found in the Red Room at Bowerhill.

Bowerhill

Miles away from the salty Kent coast, with its fortresses and oast houses, its smell of France and hops and Henry James—and even further away from Silex, The Grove, and Uncle Bertie's rabbit farm—my mother's family bred and prospered on the serene Wiltshire plains in what seems, now, to have been perpetual summer. This, of course, is because I never went there in the winter, which therefore didn't exist. Devizes and Chippenham, Trowbridge and Frome, Marlborough and Seend, were names that warmed me like the sun; and Bath near enough for a day's shopping, tea in a tearoom (with chocolate eclairs), a gulp of tepid mineral water after a visit to the disreputable Roman ruins full of steam and goldfish and smelling of old iron; shadows of clouds a mile wide moving across the empty yellow hills; Stonehenge, growing smaller and smaller every year; pink brick, trim thatch, and drifts of sheep so deep that one waded waist-high in living wool, scrunching it in one's fist, breathing heat.

And, in the middle of it all, its focus and purpose—Bowerhill. I have a conscious sense of mourning, which doesn't suit it at all. My grandmother's house outside Melksham was the most important place in my childhood, because I

believed it to be permanent. I was wrong. Try and rebuild
it with words.

A plain stone façade, decorated with a veranda under
which there were pots of fuschia and geraniums, drying
lavender and honesty, skeins of green raffia, bundles of
bamboo. Three long sash-windows upstairs, with scalloped
blinds to pull down against the sun, and deep wrought-iron
window boxes, painted white.

Behind this bland face, the house rambled back, growing
older, growing gables, low roofs, high roofs, some slate,
others tiled; it spread into dairies, stables, dovecots, pig
sties, all built of stone and splashed with Virginia creeper,
clematis, honeysuckle, many sorts of vine. There were two
huge gateposts, high as Roman columns, topped with stone
globes; but no gate between them. In the front of the
house, the immaculate lawn was like a lake dotted with
small islands of exact but varied shape, arranged with
lobelias, calcelarias, and dahlias; it stretched to white iron
railings, and beyond those was a sea of grass shadowed by
oak and beech and fir trees.

Behind the house, an acre of vegetable garden, enclosed
by a brick wall topped with stone slabs to make—for me—a
high pathway: peach, plum, apple, and nectarine trees
spread over the hot wall. The plots of the garden divided
by low box hedges, runner beans swarming over a pergola,
asparagus and poppies, cabbages and goldenrod, sweet
peas and peas: the vegetables seemed to flower. A slimy
green pond, a watering trough on wheels, wheelbarrows;
old George, the gardener, plodding up and down, twine

tied around the knees of his corduroys—he was the same age as my grandmother.

From the top of the wall—the corner over the pond, shady on hot days—I could look across the fields to Redstocks, my mother's mission. The wall was mine. I was told not to climb up there; they said it was dangerous; I didn't obey them.

A great many greenhouses, and frames for seedlings, and glass cloches for tender plants. I never learned about vegetables and flowers; there were too many. Cantaloupes—melon for breakfast, for lunch, for supper, melon jam, melon chutney. Quinces—tart, sweet, gritty jelly, cupboards of labeled and dated jars; the taste of it, back in Thornton Heath, exactly the same as the memory. Leeks, spinach, tomatoes, rhubarb, marrows: food.

Beechwoods filling in on either side of the drive, on the shady side of the house by the stables and the worn stone mounting steps; a big, weedy pond, more of a swamp in my day, king cups, water lilies; a low stone wall crusted with ivy, easy to fall off, but it didn't matter. The darkness of the woods, creeping silent on leaf mold, stripping off sheets of moss like sticking plaster; pretending to be a giant's dentist with blocks of peat, drilling them and filling them, walking about in the giant's mouth.

On the sunny side of the house, leading from the drawing room, a conservatory stifling with the smell of geraniums and lilies; out of that into a cold, dripping place entirely enclosed by a yew tree, flagstones on the ground, a well, many ferns, nobody ever stopped there; down wet steps to the potting shed, mysterious as a laboratory with

its implements, sacks, thread of every thickness, stacked
flowerpots, seed packets, catalogues; and out into the sun
of the back yard, washing strung like bunting in the orchard, chickens squawking and hopping, the washhouse
with its great boiler over a red-hot fire. I could spend a
whole August day climbing, hunting, exploring out of doors.

But sometimes it rained. They suggested I went to play
in the Red Room, long ago the children's nursery. It was
called the Red Room because it had handsome dark red
wallpaper with a formal pattern of what may have been
flowers, very gloomy. It was a large room, on the dark side
of the house, and had many treasures, chiefly an ottoman
which, when gingerly opened, released a smell of mothballs
strong enough to make you choke. There were old tennis
rackets and old books, a vast mahogany sideboard, a table
shrouded in green serge. My brother built a model speedboat—powered, I think, with electric batteries—which was
on show in the Red Room. He must have been there as
well, for there is a photograph of us taken on the lawn, he
assumes a Maggs stance, one hand in the pocket of his
navy-blue suit, the other arm latched around me in a strangle hold I can clearly remember; he looks about fourteen;
stern and responsible, but if it weren't for that, I would
swear he never came to Bowerhill.

The rooms in the front of the house had, like its façade,
quite a different character from the rest. The dining room
and drawing room opened on to the veranda: They were
not mysterious, though full of interest. As I remember my
grandmother, she didn't move about much. She seemed to
live in the dining room most of the time, which was sunny,

comfortable, and perhaps a little shabby. Here were the family portraits, my great-grandfather and grandfather, dead ancestors when unbelievably young; and my favorite, which took up most of the wall (above a cane sofa with plump green cushions), of three of my uncles as small boys, wearing sailor suits and arranged around a neat sand castle with a stiff little flag on the top, this tableau set on a vast and glistening beach with, perhaps, a few fishing boats in the distance.

Next to the bellpull—embroidered, like every cushion, tablecloth, tea cozy, and fire screen in the house, by my grandmother—there hung an oblong piece of cedarwood on which was engraved—I think with a poker—this simple message:

> So many gods, so many creeds,
> So many paths that wind and wind,
> While just the art of being kind
> Is all the sad world needs.

I read it over when I was angry with my grandmother for ordering me about: It was more of a challenge than a comfort.

The stairs that my mother came down when she was first going to meet my father; the bucket chair—on which he left his tweed hat—still in the hall. I remember going up the stairs more often than down, because there was a stained-glass window at the top, partitioning the front of the house from the rambling back; sitting on the other side of it, looking down, you could choose whether you would have a yellow, red, or blue hall, a yellow, red, or blue mother hurrying out of the dining room and down the pas-

sage, a yellow, red, or blue visiting relative coming through
the front door, to be avoided. A long time could be spent up
there, changing the color of the world. And there was the
smell of the lavatory that had only fairly recently been
built on this landing—resined wood and Jeyes' Fluid, like a
hospital in the Rocky Mountains.

But if you resisted the stained glass, you went on up an
elegant spiral to bedrooms seldom visited and never, within
my memory, used: the room my mother had slept in as a
young woman, large and light, tidy and dead. I didn't like
going up there. Unlike the rest of the house, that floor
didn't seem to belong to me.

Behind the stained-glass window the stairs switchbacked
up and down, passing my grandmother's bedroom and the
mighty, dark spare room where my mother now slept.
These bedrooms had double communicating doors, presumably so that either husband or wife could lock the other
out; they both had four-poster beds with canopies, and a
lot of furniture for resting on during the day. Eventually,
on a back landing—where the portrait of Gladstone had
been relegated, to glower only at maids and children—the
stairs divided; one half going down, black as a mineshaft,
to the kitchen quarters, the other half spindling up to the
maids' bedrooms, which had flowered wallpaper and
smelled powerfully of scented soap. At this crossroads,
where the ceilings were low and the floor covered in dark li-
noleum stamped with fleurs-de-lys, were my bedroom, the
bathroom, and high linen cupboards, which were always
kept locked.

The bathroom, of course, was a converted bedroom—

large, sunny, with a bath in the corner like the afterthought
it was. My bedroom, on the other side of the landing,
seemed like a cave. There were curtained shelves behind
the bed head, which were frightening: Hands came stealth-
ily between the curtains at night, hovering to strangle me;
the curtains moved, twitched, bulged, I was in constant
danger. Opposite my bed was a narrow doorway and yet
another spiral of stairs leading to an attic where apples were
stored in straw. I felt they were my own, personal hoard;
anyone coming to fetch apples must pass me first. I sat by
my open window with my red Gramophone, and played
"You're the Cream in My Coffee" and "All of Me," beginning vaguely to yearn for something.

   During one lunch or teatime (if teatime, there were
boiled eggs in silver egg cups) I asked, just by the way,
"Who was Oscar Wilde?" There was a frozen silence; then
the answer appeared to be that George must bring some
more melons for breakfast. After the meal, my mother
walked me up the drive. It must have cost her a lot, but she
said, "You must never mention that man in public, dar-
ling." "Why not?" "Because he was bestial." "Why?" "Because he did things with men that only ought to be done
with women." She was incapable of saying what things. I
was very confused. Shortly afterward, my father gave me a
copy of De Profundis, which I read with sympathy and
pleasure.

   There is a sad, revealing photograph taken about this
time, on which my mother wrote "The Fletcher Family":
It shows my mother, sitting in the rockery at Bowerhill,
looking ill and thin and a good deal older than she would

in twenty years' time; myself, aged about nine, grinning and squinting; and Bertie's gift, the unlovable Galahad. My father and brother were not, it seems, part of the family. There are no pictures of the four of us, and I am sure that none were ever taken.

Unlike Nellie, my grandmother Charlotte had grown smaller and more fragile with the incessant exercise of motherhood. Unlike Nellie, she had always had men of all sizes to depend on. To me, she was always extremely old: a wisp of a woman, with sparse white hair braided in a coronet above a forehead so fragile that it actually, physically disintegrated before one's eyes. This deep cavity between her temples fascinated me as much as Nellie's wart; it seemed that her head had been dead for some time, and that one day the tissue of skin would fall away, revealing a hollow skull. She had deep-set eyes, with darkness behind, like a skull; in her very old age she became blind and wore heavily tinted glasses, which more than ever convinced me that she was a tiny skeleton in clothes. The clothes were very elegant: long, dark, rustling dresses, fichus of lace or muslin, lavender silk scarves, straw hats piled high with net and artificial flowers, rings on her fingers and cameos at her throat. The flesh on her face and hands—the only parts of her I ever saw naked—had dissolved long ago; she was composed of skin, bones, and considerable spirit.

I sometimes climbed up on her high bed, in which she lay like a tiny, shriveled child, and read to her the passage of the day from a small green book called *The Cloud of*

Witnesses. But on the whole I was a nuisance to her, and I think she found me, as she did my father, noisy, ill mannered, and difficult. When I bothered her I would be sent away on some errand, given a job to do ("Satan makes work for idle hands," she would say, and "There's no such word as can't")—I was told to slide the dead pods from the dried honesty, or plait the sticky raffia, or sort out the drawer in which she kept her skeins of colored wools and silks for embroidery; I was sent to fetch her spectacles or take a message to George in the vegetable garden. Grandmother Charlotte was the only person to whom I remember shouting the clarion cry of all healthy children—"I'm not your *servant!*"—followed by a satisfactorily slammed door, and terror.

While we were at Thornton Heath, the miniature old lady appeared to live alone at Bowerhill, except when my mother and I were there. Most of the maids and cooks, whose lives from childhood to old age were spent in her service, had cottages and husbands and children in the lane that led from Spa Road to the drive; George lived in the Lodge, a whimsical little building at the gates. But there was hardly a day, it seemed, when sons, daughters-in-law, and grandchildren didn't call by; and Uncle Will came to lunch on Fridays.

Uncle Will, my mother's eldest brother, heir to the rope business, was put to work by his father at the age of sixteen, traveling the country as a salesman. Ten years later, he took over, and turned the firm into a limited company.

At the outbreak of World War I he went to India with the Wiltshire Territorial Regiment, in which he was a major. It was an important move for rope.

The laboring, working, or lower classes had for centuries used coconut matting in their cottages, but the rest of the English world knew it only as door mats. My Uncle Will foresaw a return to the simple life. During his leaves in India, he negotiated with Indian firms on the Malabar coast, and when the war was over he built an efficient factory at Allepey, which was the world center for the production of coconut fiber. For the next ten years he spent every winter in India, organizing the native labor and expanding his trade. In the summers he returned to Wiltshire, living in what seemed to me some splendor in comfortable houses with spaniels, benignly ruling his factory by the canal, and coming to Bowerhill for lunch on Fridays.

The rope factory was as magical to me as any place— tower or forgotten castle, palace above the clouds—that I read about in fairy stories. It was, to begin with, a small town: Looking down from the bridge, one watched children playing in the huge, flagged yard, women bustling in and out of cottages, the mongoloid boy—still affectionately known as the village idiot—nodding his great head in the sunshine. To go down there, to be among them, was (a little fearfully) to descend to another world.

But first, a wooden walk, built over a chasm, led from the bridge to the entrance of the factory. Standing on this, or on the pavement, one could squint up to the highest window and see the madwoman, the harmless Mrs. Rochester, peering out. She copied one's every gesture: stick thumbs into the corners of one's mouth, waggle the fingers, make terrible gargoyle faces—she would copy exactly; thumb a nose, jump up and down, she did so too behind the grimy window, grinning with delight. Inside the factory, it was a long climb to her eyrie, up rickety wooden stairs, and treacherous open stairs, and finally a ladder to a hatch in the floor: We (I distinctly remember my brother here) scrambled up with pleasurable terror, poked our heads through the hatch, saw her in the gloom winding and winding rope around great wooden spools; slithered down again, giggling with fear.

It was dark and warm inside the factory; a thick, warm smell of hemp and dust. There were mountainous bales of matting to climb on, rows of looms stretching into the distance. Many of the men who worked these looms— treadling and shuttling, friendly to an inquisitive child— were the fourth generation of Maggs workers: Gerrish, Gale, Chivers, Harvey, Guley, their skin rough as fiber, caps squarely set on their heads, stumps of Woodbines behind their ears. One of them had an interesting foot, at least six inches longer than the other, encased in an immense black boot.

Outside, on an open space between the factory and the canal, was the Ropewalk. Here, men with great pouches full of hemp walked slowly up and down, feeding hemp to the taut, singing ropes that snapped it up and somehow, by some mystery, whirled it around itself. I crawled under the vibrating ropes and got my hair caught; the whole operation had to stop while I was disentangled, and probably half a mile of good rope was ruined. I was never scolded in the rope factory. I always felt privileged. Everybody thought of me as a Maggs.

In the office, where Uncle Will presided, there were high desks with high stools, a photograph of Uncle Will in a rakish solar topi in the center of a group of his Indian workers, a number of paintings of the Malibar hills. There were even quill pens, though perhaps these were kept for sentimental reasons. I never told him how wonderful I thought the factory was: but I wish, now, that I had.

He was a mild man, with a bald brown head sprinkled with freckles, a small military mustache, and my mother's bright, hooded eyes. In his spare time and in his retirement he painted very careful oils and water colors of the Indian landscape. I sometimes sat and watched the tiny cattle being painted in on a bridge over an Indian river, jungle climbing up on either side, a patch of furred blue sky. One day his car rolled down the hill outside his house and plunged noiselessly into the village pond, where it lay submerged and unsuspected for several months. That is all I remember about Uncle Will, except for the fact that he was divorced.

He was divorced, I know now, because his wife, a romantic person named Mabel, couldn't bear to leave Malibar and her pack of white Pekinese: There was nothing really immoral about it. The only acquaintance I had with Mabel was through a huge portrait in the Red Room, a lady in white muslin and leghorn hat, rather disdainfully holding her little son Charles on her lap and looking aristocratic. In the most English way possible, she went native. Will and his son were left to fend for themselves.

This problem was either solved or further complicated shortly before my grandmother's death by his marriage to a woman I disliked for no better reason than that the entire family disliked her, except, of course, my father. There's no getting away from the fact that the Maggs were snobs, and while it's true that my step-aunt's appearance, voice, manners, and habits were unattractive, I don't think anyone bothered to investigate her actual character. It was enough for them that she had broken into the family in the guise of my grandmother's nurse; and that the lonely Will, wandering the house at night . . . and not only Will, but my father too . . . she had her evil eye on both of them, nothing better than a . . .

My step-aunt, with total lack of serenity but a strong purpose, battled through. Vulgar as she was—indeed, "common"—she married the eldest son, his rope business, his comfortable house, his painting, and his spaniels. My mother, I think, grew quite fond of her in the end. And after that, Uncle Will no longer came to lunch on Fridays, quietly presiding at the head of the table and then snoozing for precisely ten minutes in the big rattan armchair before walking the mile back to the office; and we must have missed him.

Charles, the only child of Will and the capricious Mabel, was a very romantic character to me—tall, blond, bony, and gentle, with an air of melancholy which, like many other things, I may have imagined. He was considerably older than I, and very seldom seen; but I fell in love with my image of him, and for a short period, at school, carried his photograph in the breast pocket of my blazer,

shamelessly spreading the unlikely story that he was my
boy friend. He was known in the family as Laddie, which
can't have helped his self-confidence much, and spent considerable time in India, presumably overseeing, or overlooking, the hemp. I heard that he, too, had gone a touch native; that he disappeared into the mountains and talked to
the wogs and behaved rather oddly for the son of a major.
Perhaps he found other uses for hemp than ropes and door
mats. Anyway, I was reading a book called *Scag, Son of
Power* in which this handsome young man communes with
elephants, and hypnotizes tigers when he finds himself in a
pit with them, and loves snakes and all living things, even
Indians; and I was reasonably convinced that Scag was my
cousin Laddie and would bear me off one day to a house-
boat on the Ganges, where we would wear white duck and
be fanned with ostrich feathers and invite maharajahs to
tea, surrounded by the hazy green mountains and purple
mists of Uncle Will's paintings. I shall always be grateful
to him for stirring my imagination, and what I supposed in
those days was my heart.

My Uncle Joe was the milk mogul, and my mother had
been in love with him all her life. He was her ideal man—
slow, reliable, taciturn, dressed in tweed knickerbockers
and golfing socks and highly polished brown leather shoes.
He looked curiously as Joe E. Brown must have looked
when asleep, and he was as undemonstrative as it is possible for a human being with arms and hands to be—the exact opposite, in every way, of my father. One day, seeing
him walking across my grandmother's lawn, I was over-
come by the desire to be loved by this paragon and raced

toward him, flinging myself at him with all the vigor and passion of a ninety-pound puppy. He resisted the attack by doing nothing at all, remaining perfectly still, as perhaps he had been taught to do when hunting ferocious animals. I had made a fool of myself again. He continued his walk, to inspect the condition of the white paint on the railings.

I was convinced that he had personally delivered pints of pasteurized milk to every doorstep in London, and silver-wrapped cheese and butter to every larder. He owned hundreds of sheep and miles of downland for them to graze on. He was seldom without his Irish setter, which came to heel, sat, fetched, and lived in a kennel like any properly raised dog, but completely unlike my father's. He lived with his wife, Ada, in a mellow thatched manor house that modestly presided over a village of mellow thatched cottages, all of which belonged to Joe. He was, I believe, a generous landlord, providing indoor sanitation and even bathrooms for his flock. He was a man of his word. When my mother married, he swore not to speak to her husband for twenty years. This was not difficult, as my father seldom braved Wiltshire. However, at the first opportunity after February 8, 1930, Joe uttered words in his brother-in-law's direction: They may have been "Good morning" or "Pass the port"; they were certainly not "Are you happily married?"

Ada. Aunt Ada, for some reason, terrified me. She, too, was generous (it was she who bought the chocolate eclairs in Bath), but in some indefinable way "posh." My mother wore her castoff clothes and seemed disgustingly grateful. She had carefully coiffured blond hair, and maintained a

standard of living that bewildered me. At lunch with Aunt
Ada, I was presented with a finger bowl. I had no idea
what to do with it, or what it was for. It might as well have
been a bidet. The sensible solution—to ask—was beyond
me. I burst into tears and was hurried from the table by my
mother, flushed with shame. At the manor, of which Aunt
Ada was the Lady, there were tennis parties for "the young
people" and alcoholic drinks, and pageants and scavenger
hunts, and red sports cars snorting up the gravel: in one
way or another, a painful place for a child with a tempestuous nature, heavy spectacles, and a chronic cold in the head.
It was a far cry from Uncle Bertie's rabbit farm, and made
me feel insignificant and clumsy.

There were, however, flaws in Joe's perfection; if I had
known more about them, much of my awkwardness might
have turned to grace. He had "a weakness" (so it was described to me) for the ballet, and reserved a box for every
performance of a Covent Garden season. This fact, like
Uncle Will's painting, throws a whole new light on the
family. But it is not a light I can see by. Uncle Joe never
took me to the ballet, or even mentioned it in my presence;
I never saw his face softened by Tchaikovsky or his eyes
glazed at the vision of Pavlova. It is interesting to me, surprising, but meaningless.

His other "weakness," which I knew nothing about, was
an immense kindness. His favorite brother, Fred, had married Ada's sister, Ethel. Joe and Ada were childless, and
when Ethel died in childbirth, and Fred started taking
to the bottle, Joe adopted the baby, Marcus. Like the
Irish setter, Marcus was raised well and given as many priv-

ileges, probably even some austere and intangible love. He, both nephew and son, was to carry on the dairy business; he was heir to that whole milky empire. To this end, after an obligatory public school education, he was employed by our Uncle Joe, his adoptive father, as a milkman.

Or that is what I was told. Joe, a true Maggs, with his rigid belief in hard work and discipline, believed that the future King of Milk should start from the bottom and work his way up on his own merits. It was just unfortunate that Marcus didn't have the right merits, at least according to the code of a father who refused a knighthood on principle and, as a prospective employer, turned down any young man, whatever his qualifications, who appeared for an interview wearing suede shoes. For Marcus grew up to be thoroughly frivolous, with a strong resemblance to Errol Flynn and a conscience that bore no resemblance at all to Uncle Joe's. It was he who drove the red sports car, and mixed the alcoholic drinks, and flirted with the girls over deuce and thirty-love. He almost certainly wore suede shoes. He had no stamina, no stamina at all; but he did have a good time.

It's probably wiser to leave Marcus there, having it. Disgrace settled over him, accumulated, and finally obscured him entirely from view. I broke through a temporary clearing when I was about thirteen, and went to stay with him and his wife in a commuters' heaven on the Thames—I think he was "in jam" at the time. He met me at the station and suggested that we stop in a pub on the way home. I had never been in a pub before. He bought me a gin and orange. I had never drunk alcohol before. Their home was full of mock-Tudor beams, and there were little cakes of soap in a glass jar in the bathroom. Marcus looked like Errol Flynn in his later years. His wife, Sheila or Daphne or Cynthia, looked like a wife. I never saw or heard anything of Marcus again.

At least at the manor my abysmal shyness and sense of inferiority were brought on by grownups who might have seemed alarming to the most normal child. But over a few hills and valleys, in the shabby, good-natured house where my Uncle Frank and Aunt Mercy lived with their two daughters, there was no such excuse. Frank, like Will and my mother, came from the more gentle, contemplative side of the family; he was a farmer and, like my mother, spoke with a slight Wiltshire burr, ending many sentences with the comprehensive phrase "and all," referring to clothes in the singular—"The clothes," my mother said all her life, "is on the line" or, more frequently, "Oh, Peggy, look what a terrible state your clothes is in!" Like my mother, he had a small brown face and didn't talk much. He was a justice of the peace, a governor of distinguished schools, a public figure, and so unassuming that I barely noticed him. Aunt Mercy talked incessantly in a rather shrill voice. She was kind, cheerful, possibly not very competent (which would have endeared her to my mother, who was very competitive with her sisters-in-law), and became, I was told, a martyr to rheumatism. There was nothing in either of these good people to frighten me. But I was more frightened in that sunny house than anywhere on my very circumscribed earth.

My two cousins, "the girls," frightened me. I'm sure they

had never frightened a soul before, or have since. They were healthy, pretty, extrovert, skillful at games and riding horses. They wore good, neat clothes and spoke in the high-pitched, clipped tones affected by the ladies of the present Royal Family. But there was no nonsense about them: They both married men with monosyllabic, yeomen names—not for them the Fitzgibbons and Cholmondeleys, the conceit of hyphens. They were simple, normal, and thoroughly nice. That, as far as I was concerned, was the trouble.

In Uncle Frank's house, at the advanced age of five or so, I wet my pants from sheer terror: They buttoned to a peculiar garment called a Liberty bodice, and, unable to extricate myself, I flung myself on a sofa, drumming my heels with frustration, streaming from eyes and nose and wet all over, until my mother came (in shame, as usual) to disentangle me. When I was a little older, while they played cards, or draughts, or sardines—simple, normal, thoroughly nice games—I would glare fixedly at a magazine (*Horse and Hound* or *Trout and Stream?*) since there were not, I think, any books in the public rooms of that house, books being neither useful nor comfortable.

The part of me that was Nellie's granddaughter and Bertie's niece felt like a changeling in my mother's family. It was impossible to answer her when she implored me to "join in." I didn't understand the language, the jokes, the rules, or the customs. Neither did my father, but that was no comfort: He was never there.

In secret, I practiced standing like the prettier of my two cousins, toes pointed slightly inward, knees pressed well

back; but my legs, too, were my father's and I merely
looked catatonic. My brother (he got on rather well with
them) told me, in an uncharacteristic burst of confidence,
how he had gone into the bathroom after this cousin had
taken a bath, and how there, in a drift of talcum powder,
were her tiny footprints—pointing, of course, inward. This
made me intensely dissatisfied with my own feet (the toes
were always crooked—I was strapped into orthopedic sandals at night), and so shy of my cousin that I could hardly
raise my eyes above her brown shins, which, in their turn,
made me repelled by my own, scarred and scabbed and,
whatever the season, the color of grime.

The only other uncle I knew at all well was Leonard, the
baby. I suppose that he was in his thirties when I was a
child, and second in command of "The Dairies." The milk
factory wasn't anything like as romantic as the rope factory, but it was very interesting. It was, for one thing,
excessively clean: The tiled floors were always being swilled
with water, the machinery glistened, everyone wore white
coats like doctors. The smell of milk in its natural state, before it has been pasteurized and homogenized and vi-
taminized, is remarkably strong and sweet; there were tor-
rents and cataracts of milk, lakes of it in vast tanks, one
could easily have drowned. In the laboratories, I was allowed to squint down microscopes (and never saw anything but milk), and in another part of the factory I
watched shining tins traveling up and down, round and
round, being mechanically filled with condensed milk,
fitted with lids, labeled, discharged down orderly shoots.

Uncle Leonard looked like Mr. Toad, and had many of his attributes. He was disagreeably married to a lady named Kitty, who refused, for over a quarter of a century, to divorce him. (*Was she a Roman Catholic convert?* The unseemly notion must come from somewhere.) He kept a mistress in another county—like all mistresses, she became a close friend of my mother's.

Leonard and Kitty had one daughter, Monica, known as Muffet. Although Leonard was so relatively young, Muffet seemed to me infinitely older than any of my other cousins. She existed remotely in an aura, not of scent or cologne, but perfume; she was sophisticated, and might quite possibly have been presented at court, wearing three white feathers on her head like a horse. These wild imaginings—I hardly ever met the girl—sprang from a photograph on my grandmother's piano. It was a studio photograph, and depicted Muffet's head and shoulders, naked. (This was an artistic fad of the time. I was "taken" at the age of three, swathed to the armpits in muslin, but otherwise adorned only by a coral necklace and a drunken squint—and there were all those babies, pimpled with cold, face down on bearskin rugs.) The grace of her pose, the coy curve of her shoulder, the excellence of her shingle, entranced me. Muffet had beaux while I was still on my fourth reading of *Lorna Doone*. The extent of my awe of this mythical creature can be guessed by the fact that I never associated her for a moment with tuffets, curds, and whey, or spiders.

Jinnie was my mother's only surviving sister, and I didn't connect her with Bowerhill; as far as I was concerned, she had always been safely in Australia, married to a clergyman and proudly mothering the excessively brilliant and well-adjusted cousins, one of whom became a surgeon, the other a bishop. "Aunt Jinnie's last letter from Australia" was, for me, a dreaded event: She wrote in a clear, round script and—apart from droughts, floods, and other hazards of nature—her letters seemed burdened with success. Her children, I was told, passed all their examinations, became captains of their football and cricket teams, and believed in God. I would like to know what my mother replied: "Arthur hasn't spoken for three days/has fallen in love with the new governess/says he is going to shoot himself on Monday/and I don't know what I'm going to do about Peggy." Probably not. Nobody, except my father, ever said or wrote what they really felt; it would have been bad taste and, equally horrifying, "inconsiderate."

There was another Maggs uncle in Australia—Charlie. It seems there had been no place for him either in rope or milk, and I imagined he lived somewhere deep in the bush, with only kangaroos for company. He seemed to suffer the most terrible disasters: If a tree was going to fall, it fell on Charlie; if a bush fire was going to blaze, it burned up Charlie's crops; if foot-and-mouth disease struck, it struck first at the feet and mouths of Charlie's cattle. Not knowing him, I was heartless, and thought the news of these tragedies were jokes.

Somewhere around in Wiltshire was Uncle Fred, Marcus' father, a mysterious figure. His second wife was Aunt Esther, and one of their daughters became a nun. For some reason they very seldom appeared. In fact, apart from their photographs on the piano, I don't think I believed in their existence, until one day Aunt Esther came to Bowerhill and, in the drawing room, over tea and tomato sandwiches, pronounced the words "lavatory paper." Why I was so shocked, amused, and strangely heartened, I can't now imagine. If I had known her better, I might not have been frightened of Aunt Esther.

Finally, to finish off the family where, even in my mother's memory, it began: In my childhood there were still three great-aunts, Polly, Carrie, and Maria, unmarried sisters of my grandmother's, living in exquisite timelessness and acrimony in a pretty little house called Lease Cottage on the Melksham canal. They were so old, so delicate and wizened, that I can hardly believe they were ever conscious of me. Even at the age of eight or nine, their front door seemed to me tiny, their lattice windows out of an Advent Card, their little teacups and cakes so minuscule that they belonged in a doll's house. Carrie was the smallest, Maria the roly-poly fattest, Polly the eldest. They made a noise like mice.

After my grandmother died, Leonard took over Bowerhill and, as far as my mother and I were concerned, destroyed it. Having finally got his divorce, he married his best friend's wife—not the distant mistress—and filled Bowerhill with noisy people, booze, the Savoy Orpheans and bathrooms. He installed a billiard room, and on my only visit there I remember dozing on the sofa after dinner, half listening to the click of the polished balls knocking each

other on the green baize, opening one eye to see my Uncle
Leonard, in evening shirt sleeves, ferociously chalking the
end of his cue. None of us ever stayed there again.

Foresight has no place in this story, because some of us
are still living, and don't know what will happen tomorrow; the rest are dead and, I hope, don't care. But places
are different. Chilton is still alive. If I am homesick for it I
can, physically, go back. The vicarage, the church, the
squire's mansion, the ungainly Village Club are all there;
even one of Farmer Coles's hay wagons, green as a sunken
ship, lies where it fell perhaps half a century ago.

But don't go to Melksham. There's nothing left. God
knows how many industries sprawl, how many arterial
roads get knotted, how many One Ways and No Entries
there are. There is a sign to Redstocks, pointing up a
broad, tarmacked highway. The High Street and the market square, lost in the middle of a factory city, seem derelict and afraid. The bridge has been replaced, the rope factory torn down, and the ropewalk, the cottages, the flagged
yard where the mongoloid boy nodded in the sun, look, as
I write this, like a devastated battlefield.

I don't know whether Bowerhill still stands in its gardens. The trees have been cut down and, without land-
marks, it is impossible to find. I loved it all more than I
loved people.

In the Third Place

Soon after we arrived at Thornton Heath, my mother—she must have been about fifty-three—began to suffer from appallingly heavy and almost continuous periods. I was quite old enough to sympathize. She told me that the reason she was so weak, and couldn't walk very far, was that she had chilblains. I didn't take chilblains seriously.

Perhaps it was at this time that she stopped coming up to say good night to me, and would clap her hands from the bottom of the stairs, calling "Lights out!" in her fluting voice. I resented this savagely. I banged my hand, hard, against the bed head, howling that I was injured and that she *had* to come. I know now that those stairs, and the furious child at the top of them, must have been the last straw. But if she had confided in me, or pretended to rely on me, I would have been all sweetness.

Even her rigorously inhibited temper began to get frayed. An old woman came to the front door, selling sprigs of white heather for sixpence. I asked my father, sitting in the gloom of his tiny study, to give me sixpence. He did, and I danced into the kitchen, waving my silly sprig and crowing. My mother threw down her rolling pin and screamed at me (was it a scream? was it a shout? I never heard it before or since, and was too shocked to distinguish

the exact pitch and tone of that terrifying noise)—"You!"
she screamed or shouted. "You *always* get what you want!"
I am sure that she frequently wept in the privacy of her
bedroom—the one really elegant room in the house—and
that her dead friends were a disappointment to her. Apart
from our holidays at Bowerhill, there could have been very
little to relieve her loneliness. She had, of course, planted
roses and fed the scrappy earth with the droppings of every
horse that slowly clopped up the street. But even gardening, during this time, must have been difficult.

This wretched state must have lasted for almost two
years, getting progressively worse—or, as far as I could tell,
the chilblains got worse. My father sat at his desk with his
head in his hands. I was vaguely conscious of some kind of
despair, and frequently promised to be good in future.
Then one evening, after she came toiling up the stairs in
answer to my frantic howls, my legs shot out from under
the bedclothes and I kicked her in the stomach. I remember it precisely, rage and frustration releasing springs
in my knees, both legs together; and she doubled up, saying
nothing.

The next morning I went off to school, probably buying
my pennyworth of gobstoppers, spending the day mooning
over Dr. Kaufmann, venturing valiantly toward the goal I
had set before me, whatever it was. When I came back, my
mother was in hospital. I thought I had killed her.

It was a long time before I knew that she had already
planned to go into hospital that day for a curettage.
Nobody explained. Because I couldn't confess that I'd

kicked her, I couldn't confess to the murder. I went to see her once—at the Florence Nightingale Hospital for Diseased Gentlewomen—and knew she was dying, and that she would never betray me. On the way back, I had to stop off and buy some milk. Somebody—my father?—had actually asked me to do something responsible. I remember sitting on the bus thinking that I should never see my mother again, and that I must remember to buy the milk. It was one of the rare occasions in my life when past, present, and future seemed to fit together into a coherent whole.

But she returned from hospital, and lay in bed—I think Aunt Ada came to look after us, though it seems improbable. One evening, I got back from school to find a new brown trunk in the alcove in my mother's bedroom. It had "P. R. Fletcher" stenciled on the lid, and was neatly packed with new clothes—all of them, I discovered a few days later, marked with Cash's name tapes. The decision to send me to boarding school must have been taken weeks before. I suppose you don't have to tell a doll what plans you have for its future; but a doll wouldn't have made a scene, and perhaps my mother was frightened.

She needn't have been. I was sad to leave the New School and dearest Dr. Kaufmann—though he had betrayed me anyway, by marrying Wilmay Ward's governess —but I wasn't at all sad to leave Thornton Heath. The fact that the school I was to go to was run by my unrelated Aunt Flo—my mother's companion in Norway over twenty years before—didn't impress me much. Aunt Flo was ugly, covered in freckles, and had little charm.

"BLENCATHRA"
Marine Drive, Rhyl

HOME SCHOOL FOR GIRLS

Principal. . . . Miss Florence Hiley

Assisted by Resident (4) and Visiting Teachers

Aim: To give thoroughly practical Education and to produce refined and cultured gentlewomen.

School Course: Modern, based upon all requirements for usual
Exams. Special attention to Languages, Music, Drawing, Nee-
dlework, Physical Exercise, Health of Pupils.

Special provision for delicate or backward girls. *Entire charge
taken of Pupils whose Parents are abroad.*

Premises face Sea; sheltered position; Electric Light; perfect
Sanitation. Bathing from House. Playing Field (games).

Rhyl The Medical Officer of Health writes: A first-class watering place, having 2 miles of seaboard. Promenade. Well sup-
plied in matters of sanitation. Rainfall below the average and a
sunshine record one of the best in the kingdom. Climate dry,
bracing and sunny.

This was my destination when I was put into a railway
carriage at Euston—in charge of the Guard, I'm sure—and
sped happily (one usually remembers grief, and I don't) to
Crewe, where I was met by Aunt Flo. I was enraptured by
the prospect of Crewe, since there was in those days an advertisement depicting a desperate lady in a cloche, surrounded by suitcases and bewailing, "Oh, Mr. Porter, what
shall I do? I was reading *Everybody's* and got carried on
to Crewe!" Crewe, like Valhalla, Delphi, or Troy, was
therefore part of a myth—but I didn't see much of it. We
changed trains, and went on a very long way to Rhyl, my

Aunt Flo's gloved hand holding mine and stroking it with her scratchy thumb until the skin was sore. She probably did this to reassure me, but it was very uncomfortable.

I don't know how many potentially refined and cultured gentlewomen there were at Blencathra—probably not more than thirty. They seemed to me an enormous crowd, but I don't remember being afraid, even though at my first meal I was gently reprimanded for not holding my fork properly. I slept in a dormitory, about which I remember nothing except looking in the mirror and wondering whether, if I really put my mind to it, I could manage to look like Greta Garbo—I had yet to see her on the screen, but was an avid reader of film magazines and thought her pictures were awesomely beautiful.

I was happy at Blencathra. In the winter, the sea raged and we stood around the piano and sang "Eternal Father Strong to Save," piping up against the storm. In the summer, we dressed up and performed plays in the garden. I suppose we bathed in the sea and played on the beach, but were probably too regimented for it to be memorable. I learned how to sew on buttons, and how to behave properly at table in case Princess Elizabeth asked me to tea—the extreme improbability of this fantasy—or threat—didn't disturb me. I adored an older girl, called Betty Rhodes, and took a picture of her with my new box camera, dressed up in a Fair Isle sleeveless pull-over, gray flannel bags, and hair scraped unbecomingly behind her ears.

I decided that the next term, when I would be properly established and respected at Blencathra, my mother should come and visit me. I knew that the fare from London to

Rhyl must be astronomical, and doubted whether she could afford it. All the spring term, and all the Easter holidays, I secretly hoarded my pocket: At last I was able to send her a ten-shilling note, and ordered her to come immediately.

She agreed, and a date was set. I felt sick with excitement, planning how I would show her my secret haunts (I must have had some—the urge for a Bath-hound was still very strong), and thinking how she would be there, in the next room perhaps, while I did my lessons and when I went to bed at night. I was proud of Blencathra and proud of myself. I wanted to make her proud of me, and for her to have a nice time for once.

She arrived, and spent most of her stay closeted with Aunt Flo, knitting. The visit was a deep disappointment. She didn't even thank me for having paid her fare. I was a nonentity. She hadn't come to see me at all. Perhaps this was the most important part of my "thoroughly practical Education" at Blencathra; but, unlike sewing on buttons, it seemed useless for many years.

At the end of that term, Aunt Flo came into our dormitory one night and sat on my bed. She said that Blencathra was closing down, and that in May I would be going to a new school in Buckinghamshire—an amazing school where, believe it or not, I would be able to do exactly as I liked. I wouldn't have to go to lessons if I didn't want to, or wear uniform, or keep any rules. It sounded to me as though it just might approach the joy of my day with Uncle Bertie, but Aunt Flo's voice must have been a little hollow as she described it to me. It was not her idea at all of how to produce a refined and cultured gentlewoman.

I was sad that Blencathra was closing. Everything
seemed very temporary. The Little People's Garden had
come and gone. I had learned to play the recorder at the
New School (a pang for Dr. Kaufmann) and then been sent
to a place where there were no recorders. I had learned to
sew on buttons at Blencathra, and was now being sent to a
place where, from the sound of it, there were no buttons.
Still, the new school sounded hopeful; and I must be growing responsible, for my father actually sent me a prospectus
of it, with photographs. Optimistic, swaggering a little, I
felt sorry for those girls who were being sent off to learn
fractions and French verbs in dull establishments named
for forgotten saints.

In the Fourth Place

We may have spent the Easter holidays at Bowerhill, or we may have spent them in a place called Milford, where I think there was a holiday house or home for needy vicars. If it was Milford, my mother made the acquaintance of a new family of ghosts. If it was Bowerhill, this may have been the spring when I fell in love again, with a boy who operated a roundabout at the fair. He always wore a canary-yellow pull-over, and I would bicycle to the fairground before breakfast in the hope of seeing him. I'm pretty sure we never spoke. He must have been about fifteen, and stood nonchalantly on the whirling carousel, not even holding on.

I do know that the holidays were made particularly glorious by the fact that we were leaving Thornton Heath, though I didn't realize that this was related to my father's sudden and catastrophic discovery of communism. Bored with the afterlife, his energy had soared once more. With his usual reckless enthusiasm, he had devoted a whole issue of the parish magazine to supporting the Soviet persecution of the Church. Christ, he argued, was the first communist; Lenin and Marx (I'm not sure about Trotsky) were true apostles; the Church (Orthodox or Anglican, they were all the same) was corrupt, decadent, and immoral, and should immediately be disbanded. He himself would be the first to turn St. Peter's, Thornton Heath, into a museum or cinema or even garage, if one were needed.

Nobody understood it. He was appalled, amazed. At last, after so much searching, he had rediscovered Christianity. Did the Church of England not care for Christianity? Apparently not. He had been advised to leave the diocese, and we were moving to Derbyshire, which, for us, was the North. Perhaps a little money had come from somewhere, because my mother was full of plans for stair carpets, and my brother was mistakenly asked to design my bedroom furniture, which would be made by a local carpenter and painted—according to my tasteless instructions—apple green.

There was also the Garden School, Lane End, near High Wycombe, Bucks, to look forward to; and, although I didn't know it then, my first experience of prolonged distress.

I'm sure the Garden School meant well. It was, at that time, the wrong place for me. At the age of eleven, in spite of my poetry and prancing and carrying on, I was as firm a Wesleyan, at heart, as my father. The New School, for all its outlandish beliefs, had been domestic and tranquil as a nursery; at Blencathra, table manners and genteel courtesies hadn't been too hard to learn. When I found myself in a place where the convention was to be "free" and artistic and troublesome, where everyone else was "difficult"— and probably selfish and ungrateful as well—I didn't know what to do; I was lost.

As I wasn't required to go to lessons, I wandered around

among the mangy rabbits and cats for a few weeks, the mud (it was a wet summer, and fashionable to go barefoot) squelching between my toes. After that, for shelter, I crept into whatever class I could find, whether it was seventeen-year-olds studying Comparative Religion or five-year-olds pounding clay. Rabindranath Tagore visited and, since I was passing, blessed me. It didn't do any good. A'Lelia, the pretty daughter of a famous black entertainer called Layton, shared my dormitory with about six other girls and two snoring spaniels. A'Lelia played her father's records late into the night, when I knew perfectly well I should be tucked up and asleep. I desperately wanted to be cared for, and to have somebody to tell me that I was full of sin.

I was probably bored for the first time in my life. I wrote passionate letters to my parents insisting that I wanted to *work*, to *learn* something, to be *useful*. I said I wanted to be like my brother, and be *educated*. My mother was directing the carpet layers in Belper; my father, temporarily chastened, was starting a new life. But they came to visit me, and may have had plaintive conversations with the headmistress; when they left, I cried, it seemed, for the rest of the term.

Now they had moved to Derbyshire—which surely must be more like the country than Thornton Heath—I wanted to go to day school again. I had a fantasy of setting off each morning with my satchel, getting my own breakfast; I saw myself sitting at a desk, uniformed, learning beautiful facts, shooting up my hand to answer every question; I imagined coming home, quietly doing my homework, helping my mother, being a solace to her. I was, in fact, confused.

I think they did go and look at a few day schools in and around Belper. But the prospect of having me at home all the time must have appalled them. Neither of them was capable of making a habit of loving: To my mother, it was a threat, a disruption, something to be kept at bay; to my father, love was loud and operatic, with many intervals. Ordinary old love, taking and leaving, snapping and hugging, yawning while watching a child grow, was outside their experience. St. Elphin's School for the Daughters of the Clergy, Darley Dale, near Matlock, was cheap and respectable. The Bishop of Bradford's daughter was head girl. I would be near enough to be fetched without too much expense and trouble, and far enough away not to disturb their afternoon sleep. And if I really wanted to be like other girls, and pass examinations, I might manage to become a hospital nurse.

So I was allowed to leave the Garden School, and was taken in A'Lelia's father's gray Rolls-Royce (I was sick on its silver upholstery) to London and put on a train for Derby. My father met me in a new car, and I began to get the feeling that we were wealthy, people to be reckoned with. When we drove up the drive to the vicarage—a big, solid house, plain, with no pretensions—I remembered Thornton Heath, and yelped with joy. My mother, for some extraordinary reason, was sitting on the stairs—perhaps the final rods were being laid on the carpet. I raced from room to room. There was space again. The familiar furniture had regained its dignity and there were huge new armchairs, more like small sofas. I admired my modernistic, apple-green bedroom and ran out to explore the garden. It was big, there were secret places, disused stables, a sloping lawn. The sky may have been a bit gray, and the air a bit dank, but my mother seemed so happy and chatty that I knew it must be a great step in the right direction— back to Chilton, Bowerhill, our own kind of place.

Belper is a manufacturing town—sewing thread and, in those days, silk stockings. It wasn't very attractive, but it was busy, and I had never lived in a provincial town before. The river Derwent slugs through it, banked by municipal gardens and cotton mills, and St. Peter's, my father's church, seats fifteen hundred people, few of whom were ever there. Another of the myriad things I didn't know was that Belper, England, and most of the world, were well into the Great Depression. In fact, I thought for some time that this term had something to do with Sunday afternoons. There must have been an overwhelming number of unemployed in Belper, compared with the well-to-do solicitors, estate agents, mill owners, and shopkeepers who supported the town's three Anglican churches, one Roman Catholic church, and the Congregational, Baptist, and Unitarian chapels. I must assume that some of these people cared, and I'm sure my father did, in his way. It would be surprising, too, if my mother hadn't hit on some scheme for providing children with homemade toffee or teaching their distraught mothers how to do macramé. But I was not informed. Therefore, as usual, I did not know. Nobody ever impressed on me that the only way to learn anything, in school or out, was to ask questions. Even if they had, I would have needed information about what questions to ask. The whole business of learning was, therefore, a vicious circle.

On my twelfth birthday, my parents took me to St. Elphin's, delivered me to the Junior School, and went away. I was square, flat-chested (which my father commented on, critical, his fierce little eyes trying to bore through my school jersey), beginning to be spotty, glasses askew over my squint, a wide grin at the slightest thing worth grinning at. My straight hair was still clasped by the mechanical barrette: I was not a pretty child.

This part of the Midlands, from Harrogate down through Buxton to Matlock, gushes mineral springs: St. Elphin's had originally been built as a hydropathic hospital, a place pungent with potted palms and Epsom salts, where cotton millionaires could cure their gout, their palpitations, and their melancholia. In order to deal with all the linen, towels, and even perhaps winding sheets required in this business, the owners had built a laundry, with a chimney taller and blacker than that required for any laundry. The main house was—is?—an immense heap of gabled roofs, french windows, casement windows, latticed windows, bow windows, bay windows, frosted-glass windows, stained-glass windows, small apertures for servants' windows, all punctured haphazardly into brick and ivy. Inside, there were great landings and galleries, quantities of tormented oak: The Disgrace Bench, on which I was to sit for many hours sewing chapel-kneelers, was on the first landing, just outside the Staff Room and the

headmistress' study; as an even more undignified punishment, one had to sit in the hall all day, writing lines
("Stern Daughter of the Voice of God/O Duty, if thy
name we love . . ."), and no passer-by was allowed to
speak or smile. It would have been less effectively humili-
ating, I suppose, to be locked in stocks.

The original Hydro had been extended to accommodate
the two hundred or so daughters of bishops, archdeacons,
deans, rectors, and vicars (I feel sure there were no curates), who flocked from Lancashire, Yorkshire, Wales,
Cheshire, Lincolnshire, and—most plentifully—Birming-
ham. For many years these extensions had been in the
form of huts and sheds, possibly army surplus from World
War I, which had become a kind of comforting slum out
of sight of the main house. Insufferably hot in summer,
below freezing in winter, they contained dilapidated desks
and benches, blackboards gray with inerasable chalk, wilt-
ing specimens of seasonal flora, notice boards covered in
tattered baize and inextricable drawing pins. In one of
these huts, intended for "prep" or solitary study, I would
later struggle alone and, I felt, unaided with my two most
detested subjects: botany, and musical theory; and listen to
Bing Crosby records; and write the kind of poetry that
Walt Whitman might have written if he had been the
pubescent daughter of an erratic Church of England clergyman living in Derbyshire in the 1930s. I think the Art
Room was somewhere in this huddle of shacks, but when I
first went to St. Elphin's the only recognizable art in the
place was the plaster replica of the Venus de Milo in the
front hall; we bombarded it with the cascara pills that were

given us each night for the first three weeks of every term, to purge us of the impurities of home cooking.

God, of course, was much in evidence; He was not only patron of the school, but He paid the fees. The chapel, down a lugubrious path walled with rhododendron and laurel, was God's house. Tom Wolfe, in *The Painted Word*, describes how, in the Social Realist period of the thirties, painters were "dutifully cranking out paintings of unemployed Negroes, crippled war veterans, and the ubiquitous workers with open blue work-shirts and necks wider than their heads." The Chapel of St. Elphin's School for the Daughters of the Clergy was, rather astonishingly, decorated by such a painter. Instead of unemployed Negroes, there were unemployed miners; and there were unemployed miners' wives and children, all with necks wider than their heads and thick bodies without bone structure. The predominant color was blue, blue scenes of Social Realism covering every inch of wall and ceiling in the chancel, where I would soon sit in my choir stall wearing a white veil and gloves, waiting to launch into "Jesu Joy" or Stanford's Magnificat in C or some Lenten dirge (which I enjoyed more) and examining with interest these lumpish substitutes for saints. There was a wreath of wild flowers painted with an attempt at trompe d'oeil over the headmistress' carved throne; it was said that it was meant to look as though she were wearing it.

The headmistress, Miss Margaret Flood, M.A., was—though I didn't appreciate it at the time—a sane woman. God was her employer. She respected Him, read His works, carried out His orders, did a good job; but, like any efficient secretary with a life of her own outside office hours, she was not in love with Him. We were not whipped into frenzy by her passion, driven into tempests of tears by her ardor, or brought to our knees by anything more than a polite but perfunctory "Let us pray." The roses and raptures, lilies and languors, came later, with her successor, Miss Mildred Hudson, who was not sane. The girls attended chapel at least twice a day, seven days a week, wearing panama hats in summer, gray felt hats in winter—except for the choristers, and we were veiled like midget nurses or flighty nuns, and headed the twice-daily procession from the main building, one of us carrying a crimson and gold cross on a long pole.

At some time in the late twenties, the school must have benefited from an endowment and, perhaps, new blood on the Board of Governors: The Junior School, where my parents took me that first day, was relatively new. It was connected with the main building by a covered way: Once across this the walls, floor covering, the colors and smells, even the weather changed. Each of us had our own blue-curtained cubicle, our own cupboard and chest and locker; the highly polished corridor between the cubicles could be slid along from end to end, either on our sensible leather-soled shoes or—as I discovered before my first week was over—on pillows. The schoolrooms reminded me of the Little People—the same hips and haws and largely useless enterprises. We wore white pinafores over our gym tunics at mealtime, because we were expected to be clumsy with our food. They aimed at a feeling of innocent merriment, nursery tea, bedtime stories; no one thought of gentle

Jesus, meek and mild with his blond curls and Grecian tunic in an English meadow, as a boy.

For two weeks, relieved from the awful responsibilities of the Garden School, I had a wonderful time. I made the little Daughters shudder with my stories of ghosts, and girls blowing off their breasts with muskets, and playing naked on a rabbit farm. I made up tales of incredible journeys to places I had never been—India, Shangri-la, Australia, Tahiti, Brighton—and they believed every word. I told them I didn't believe in God and often went without knickers, neither of which was true. A sense of power may have taken the place of a sense of security, but the result was the same. It was a return to the Golden Age, with the added advantage of knowing (a little) what history had in store.

But they summoned me, and said I was to report to Form IVb in the Senior School; and if childhood can ever be said to end, that was the end of mine.

I approach the next few years with as much suspicion and doubt as I approached the Form IVb classroom that day, still foolishly wearing my pinafore, peering out over a load of exercise books, and my Bible and prayer book. When at last I managed to open the door, and stood hopeful and terrified, everyone burst out laughing. I wouldn't want to repeat that.

Catherine Gethen, Truda McClaren, Betty Chamberlain, Irene Wells, Ceridwen Maurice-Jones, Gwyneth Hopkins: Their gym tunics were already bulging at the seams, they whispered and tittered, rustled paper bags in the dormitory. Wendy Ellison and Cynthia Pugh: women, who wore suspender belts and brassieres, sleeveless nightdresses, curled their hair with pipe cleaners. I wore striped Vyella pajamas, and failed to keep my stockings up with garters made of black elastic.

For a long while after that, my career was an unmitigated calamity. I was frightened all the time. Miss Flood, rosy and round, terrified me; Miss Beavis, the science teacher (her eyebrows had been blown off in a scientific explosion, and she kept telling us to observe the laundry chimney—"*belching* out carbon dioxide!") terrified me; Miss Sadler, the matron, frightened me so much that I froze to attention at her approach, and was unable to speak. She was well over six feet tall, had the face of an intemperate general, and had been a nurse with the British forces at Murmansk or Archangel. As far as Miss Sadler was concerned, I was a Bolshevik. She persecuted me, hounded me, gave me the third degree. When I came back to school without a panama hat—reasonably assuming that now I was in the choir, I wouldn't need one—she told me to go straightaway, this minute, and find my panama hat. I stammered that I didn't have a panama hat. She told me to go and bring her my panama hat. I insisted that I didn't have a panama hat to bring her. She said I was lying. I whimpered that I was not lying. She hissed through her camel's teeth and gave me a conduct mark and an hour on the Disgrace Bench. I wrote to my mother, begging her to send the panama hat by return. When it arrived, folded into a neat cone, Miss Sadler said that I had ruined my panama hat and must ask my mother for a new one: She knew very well, she said, that I had been hiding my panama hat from her the whole time.

Injustice: I boiled and howled with it. We had to wear galoshes, which were kept with our outdoor shoes, lacrosse sticks and hockey sticks and tennis rackets and cricket bats, in a dreadful cellar. We automatically knocked the cockroaches out of our shoes before putting them on, and squelched the beasts underfoot. I lost my galoshes. Miss Sadler told me to go and find them. I said I couldn't find them, because they were lost. Miss Sadler said that it was impossible to lose galoshes if they were properly marked, and that if mine weren't properly marked, it was an offense. I said they were properly marked, but I had lost them. She said she knew me, I had not lost my galoshes at all, I was keeping them from her. I denied it (why was Miss Sadler so passionately fond of my galoshes?). She gave me an order mark for impertinence and an hour on the Disgrace Bench. A few days later, I found my galoshes in somebody else's locker. The relief was so immense that I burst into tears.

In the vast dining room, there were long refectory tables and a raised dais, on which sat Miss Flood, other senior mistresses, sometimes the head girl, one or two favored prefects, and the visiting clergy. Miss Flood rang a little bell for grace at the beginning and end of each meal, and in emergencies. We were not allowed to ask for things to be passed to us. I was not only below the salt, but never got any. We had tin mugs to drink out of, which made the already mineral water taste of lead. One day I found a worm in my mince. It was an authentic worm, wriggling about in the thin gravy. I screamed quite loudly. The bell rang; I was ordered out of the dining room. Miss Sadler's view was that there could not possibly have been a worm in my mince. "I've never heard of such a thing," she said. Neither had I. As a punishment, I was made to wear my Junior School pinafore to meals, to show everyone what an untruthful little pig I was.

At the beginning of my second year, I ran away.

2

My father had by now begun to suffer terribly from arthritis, sciatica, protests from his body, and was so heavy that it was increasingly difficult for him to move about. He went everywhere by car, hunched over the wheel, saluting his parishioners with a gesture that was half gracious, half insulting. His Standard or Humber or Morris (he was never satisfied, continually unfaithful) was his mistress and true companion, escaping with him to Sheffield and Nottingham, accompanying him on long, aimless drives over the moors. He was in his mid-fifties, and almost friendless.

There was a pleasant, gentle schoolmaster called Mr. Bye, who lived far away in, I think, Tunbridge Wells. My father called him Bye, and they may have corresponded a little. There was also a strange man who looked like Malcolm Muggeridge would look in a few years' time, a Machiavellian gnome. He had a Scots name, Mac-something, and was a mystery. My father said, for a short while, that he was a friend. But he assaulted a choirboy or Boy Scout, or both, embezzled the church funds (my father had made him a church warden), and disappeared. My father's fellow clergymen were, of course, impossible. The doctor was amiable, but stupid. My father was incapable of being friends with women, and in any case my mother always captured them first, stupid or smart, attractive or plain, provided they were middle class and over thirty, or working class and any age. "There's not a single intelligent person in the place," he would groan. He might as well, he said, live on a desert island.

But there was, from time to time, me. His study was thick with stale tobacco smoke. If I had to go in there (why did my mother send me? Because she didn't want to go herself), I couldn't get away. He mauled me without tenderness. One day I squirmed off his lap and ran, ran into the garden, the air. We had a tennis game, a ball on a long piece of elastic, strung from a pole. I picked up a racket and began to hit the ball in a blind fury—the ball was my father. He came out into the garden and stood watching me. His face was red and, insofar as the construction of his face allowed, simpering. I hit the ball at him, wanting to hit him; but it sprang back on the elastic, hitting me.

Using the same formidable power of his loneliness, he had begun to assault me mentally as well as physically. Perhaps "assault" sounds too strong a word for this, but any twelve-year-old who has sat, captive, for hours at a time in an airless room listening to a man who discovers a new key to the universe at least twice a week, experiences a violent verbal attack, and is assaulted. Perhaps he thought he was bringing me up; something which, according to my mother, had always been done extremely badly, leaving me little hope. I think he was using me, just as he did when he pulled me onto his knee and fumbled in my knickers. But in some ways I find it harder to forgive; I believed what he said, but knew, by now, that what he did was furtive and unworthy and indisputably wrong.

Anyway, among other things, he had told me that I must always be free, always kick against the pricks and try to demolish brick walls; never, if I wanted his (curiously mixed with Jesus Christ's) approval, toe anybody else's line. He told me that marriage was the coffin of love, that I must never suffer from false modesty, and that life was like a gas fire. I had no idea what this last statement meant, and don't now, but have a very clear picture of the gas fire and a very strong feeling of its arid heat, so perhaps he was just saying that life was hell. He told me that all the mistresses at St. Elphin's were frustrated spinsters and could never teach me how to become a woman. He told me always to follow the devices and desires of my own heart, and that God had never existed. He told me that he loved me, and that I only had to call and he would be there. At this point I would try to get away on any pretext (there weren't many), but if I was tactless about it he would plunge into a terrible raging gloom that often lasted for days; there would be notes under my bedroom door, and dark rumblings of finishing it all. I never learned to be tactful, and soon came to treat his threat of suicide as just one more unkept promise and broken vow.

But at this time, trapped for a large part of the year between Miss Sadler and Miss Flood, I was rather proud of him; even, perhaps, of his sexual eccentricities. The other

fathers of the Daughters of the Clergy were extremely dull,
however safe. They wore black and said grace and had
plaintive voices; they had puny appetites and lived in dingy
houses with photographs of their theological colleges on
the walls. When I told my few friends at school what my
father believed—I wasn't altogether truthful about what he
did—they snickered and giggled and were astounded. I felt
superior. In my intense homesickness, exiled among what
my father had assured me were spiritual foreigners, fresh
from my holiday lessons in how to be a revolutionary, I decided that the least I could do was to make him proud of
me. Therefore—and because I had been given a conduct
mark for talking after the Prayer Bell on the second night
of the new term—I ran away.

I have thought about this story so much in my life, and
written it, in various forms, so often; but it has never grown
the patina of fiction, and in whatever guise it appears it
never deviates from the implacable truth. The facts are
simple. I went to bed in the dormitory as though everything were normal: Then, when all the other Daughters
were finally asleep, I dressed myself under the bedclothes,
putting on my striped flannel shirt, navy serge skirt, and
lisle stockings. I put on my pink cotton kimono (embroidered, not printed, with parrots or flamingos) over my
clothes, and crept to the lavatory along the dim landing,
and went in and locked the door. It was a very small lavatory, on the top floor, but I thought there must be a fire escape within jumping distance, as the building was scaf-
folded with fire escapes which we used on our frequent
fire drills.

I folded the kimono and left it on the floor, opened the narrow frosted-glass window and, carrying my shoes with my teeth, squirmed out and dangled for the fire escape, which was a bit further away than I had thought. It was a foggy night. I was very excited. I thought my father would be very excited, too.

I walked to Matlock, maybe two miles, and saw two policemen standing under a street light. I asked them the way to Belper. They questioned me a little, but without enthusiasm. I said my name was Peggy Forbes (not altogether untrue—my father had recently affected the name Forbes-Fletcher, but no one could get used to it) and that my bicycle had broken down in Rowsley and I knew someone who lived on the Belper road. They showed me the way, quite friendly.

When I was outside Matlock, and realized I had about ten miles to go—the road was fairly desolate in those days— I felt a bit uneasy. The fog was quite thick. But I got a lift in a truck, and told the driver as few lies as possible. He dropped me at the bottom of the vicarage drive, and I was glad to see there was a light still on in the hall.

The front door was locked, which I hadn't expected, so I rang the bell. My father was just going to bed. I heard him walk along the hall and through the porch, and he opened the door. I had been right—he was excited. He was so excited that he stuttered, like someone wrongfully accused of murder. My mother was asleep, and he wouldn't hear of waking her up. That was when he had bustled me into the sitting room and shut the door.

I don't think it's too fanciful to say that was the first

time I realized that the world existed independently of myself. When I looked around the sitting room, I had this shocking revelation—the fire had obviously been burning all evening, my father reading, my mother knitting: The fire now nearly dead, and my mother's knitting bag was on her chair. Without my presence, let alone my permission, they had been eating, walking in and out of rooms, wearing the same clothes that they wore when I was with them, planning tomorrow, remembering yesterday. To them, it was *myself*, who didn't exist. They had a life of their own. The existence of some microscopic part of me, some fastening or delicate hinge of identity, became uncertain from then on.

I had expected that we would talk—of course he would want to know what had happened—and that then my mother would make cocoa, and I would go to bed in my apple-green room. Not a bit of it. Our conversation, if it can be called that, was an outraged interrogation: Who had seen me, whom had I told? This was followed by an incomprehensible tirade about scandal, his position as vicar of the parish, the newspapers, my mother's health, my insane lack of consideration. I began to cry, which infuriated him more. For once, I would have been grateful to sit on his knee, but he didn't touch me. He telephoned Miss Flood in dismayed apology, bundled me into my mother's gardening coat—very old, brown, Harris tweed—and drove me straight back to St. Elphin's.

We didn't talk on the way back. The police had been called out, and by that time were rapping on the vicarage door, alarming my mother, thumping about in their boots.

At school, there was a welcoming committee waiting on the steps, Miss Flood monumental in a dressing gown, a number of women I didn't look at.

When we got into the hall, I threw a small fit, clinging to my father and yelling for help. He promised that if I would be quiet, he would come and say good night to me before he left. I made him promise again, then went with a maid to a strange guest room overlooking the drive. She saw me into bed and turned off the light. I waited, and an interminable time later heard my father's car start up, the headlights swept over the ceiling, and he drove away.

There seemed to be many conferences, and a great air of trouble. Miss Flood told me, quite gently, that I had been out of my mind ("not yourself" was, I think, her strange way of putting it). The question was, whether I should be expelled or not. It seemed to me quite irrational to expel someone for running away—surely the most appropriate punishment would have been to keep me there forever?— but I realized they were not rational. My parents came once or twice—I saw the car in the drive, but was not allowed to meet them. I was never told what my mother's attitude was to it all, and I don't know why I have the feeling that she was more tolerant and less dismayed than anybody else; but I trust it. Behind her shield of appearances, she was far less conventional and tied to tradition than my father. If she had known, I think she would have made cocoa.

They decided not to expel me, but I had to sit on the Disgrace Bench every evening for the rest of the term. I sewed many chapel-kneelers. However, there were compensations. I obviously couldn't go back to sleep in the dormitory, where I might corrupt other girls. I was moved to the wing where the seniors slept in rows of little boxes, the walls not reaching the ceiling, like public lavatories. Each box had a big window, a wardrobe, a chest of drawers, and a bed; by pulling out the drawer at the bottom of the wardrobe, it was possible to block the door. I had a private place again, where I could write and read and practice looking like Greta Garbo, a few of whose films I had now seen. My father preferred Elizabeth Bergner. I gave her a try, smirking and clenching the tip of my tongue between my teeth, but it was a failure. My bath nights were on Tuesdays and Fridays and my number—we were all numbered, like convicts or soldiers—remained unchanged: 122.

Miss Flood wondered whether I should be confirmed—perhaps it might stabilize me. (My brother, still at his minor public school, had been confirmed a year or so before in Sir Gilbert Scott's eight-year-old cathedral in Liverpool. We went to the service, and seeing him kneeling at the altar rail, far away in the distance, I had been curiously moved.) Meeting me in the hall one day, she congratulated me on not bearing any malice. I didn't know what she meant, but felt absolved. If it was going to make Miss Flood happy, I didn't mind getting confirmed, though my heart wasn't in it. Luckily, I caught the measles and was taken off to the sanitorium. Miss Flood said that she didn't think I was quite "ready" for confirmation anyway.

Miss Sadler must have left by now, though I remember no roll of drums or salute of cannon at her departure. I think it was Miss Grenfell who took over, a relatively motherly person of reasonable size. The sanitorium was rather cozy, like somebody's house. I enjoyed having the measles, but didn't expect it to change my life.

One morning, when I was getting better, I rolled out of bed and wandered over to the dressing table to brush my hair. It wasn't actually a dressing table, but a high, white-painted chest of drawers with a mirror standing on it. I suppose I glanced in it with my usual pessimism—no Garbo, no Bergner—and was immediately terrified. My reflection had straight eyes. I wasn't squinting. I yelled for Miss Grenfell, who came bustling and rustling in her nurse's uniform. I stared at her, shouting, "Look, look!" She had no patience with me. "Your eyes are always straight when you wake up in the morning, dear. Now hurry up, breakfast's ready."

I ran to the mirror every ten minutes that day: still straight. Next morning I approached it cautiously, hoping to catch it out: Two obedient and perfectly balanced eyes stared back at me. At the end of the week, I threw away my glasses and emerged, at last, as my idea of a girl.

3

It was not so much that the world no longer saw me wearing glasses; it was the fact I no longer saw the world through glass that changed my view of things. Since my third birthday, my face had been dressed in wire and steel. Now, suddenly, it was naked. I cut myself a fringe with my

sewing scissors, and threw out the barrette. I planned to become something I had not thought I could ever be—flighty.
As I still weighed a good ten stone, this was an unlikely
ambition.

I had, as we all had, many remote objects of passion:
Gary Cooper, Inigo in Priestley's *Good Companions* (the
character, as much as young John Gielgud in the film),
many film stars whose names I forget—but they were all
blond and bony, brave and shy—and, because of his liquid,
almost edible eyes, Conrad Veidt. I certainly suffered and
sighed over some older girls at school, though don't remember who they were. When I went home for the holidays, the doctor's youngest son remarked that I was quite
pretty.

His name was Denis, and he was at school with my
brother, though very junior to him—perhaps he was even
my brother's "fag." I had first met him coming off the
school train in a welter of dropped luggage and clumsy
greetings; he was about fifteen, with huge, unco-ordinated
hands and sticky blue eyes—infinitely prettier than I. He
and his brother, Terence, both played the piano extremely
well—they had two pianos in their room, I suppose in the
hope that they would play duets. In fact, I don't think they
liked each other very much. My father allowed Denis to
play the organ in church; we would go there on weekday
evenings, and my job was to pump the bellows in a dusty
place behind the organ pipes. The electric light in the organ
loft was a bright cabin in the vast, echoing darkness of the
church. As well as Bach and Vivaldi, Denis played Gersh-

win, and the popular songs I loved. I pumped furiously, giving the instrument breath.

In the winter, we went skating together, though I couldn't really skate. Denis pulled me along behind him on a broom handle, I wore a red turtle-neck sweater. He had a motor bike, deafening, a thermos of water strapped to the pillion to throw over the engine when it threatened to blow up. I too rode the pillion, clinging like a limpet.

Shortly after my metamorphosis, we were taken to Sheffield on the train to see *Toad of Toad Hall*—there was a small group of "children," or whatever we were meant to be at that time, and somebody must have been in charge. Whoever they were, they hadn't organized the expedition well, because we had to stand in the side aisle of the theater for the whole performance. Denis stood behind me, and my back crept and tingled in a curious way. In the train coming back, we found a compartment to ourselves and fell in love, or, more accurately, together. When we got to Belper station, Denis suggested that we stay on the train until it reached Derby. It felt more like entering Eden than being cast out.

So I had a boy friend, though according to my mother that was a very "common" term. He was not very reliable, but a great occupation; the slab of blond hair which he continually pushed away from his eyes, his clumsiness and sweetness, made him for many years my model of desirability.

About this time, my mother said to someone we met in the street. "Yes, it's nice when they begin to grow up. They become more like friends." I treasured this remark, often searching for it in times of trouble.

The school year always started on, or within a few days of, my birthday. This gave me very mixed feelings about my birthday. But on or around the day I was fourteen, I went back to find a revolution had taken place. It was the only beginning of term, I think, when I was not wretchedly homesick.

Miss Flood had retired to Glastonbury, and her place had been taken by Miss Mildred Hudson. I suppose Miss Hudson was relatively young, a tall, angular woman whose hair was always falling down; she wore sturdy crepe soles to her shoes, which squeaked on the parquet, silk stockings and tweed skirts and a crucifix. She was deranged as only a nun can be deranged. But to begin with she seemed like a savior.

The whole place gleamed with fresh paint, there were muted prints hanging on the walls, and the tin mugs had been replaced by glass tumblers. The Disgrace Bench had gone, and there was electric light in the labyrinthine passages, which previously had been gloomily lit with gas jets. There were a number of new teachers—young, bobbed women recently down from Girton or Lady Margaret Hall. They strode about the place in a boyish manner, smoked cigarettes in the Staff Room, and sometimes became hysterical. One of them was Sheila Mary Taylor, whose job it was to drum Wordsworth and *The Merchant of Venice* into our dizzy heads. She was the first person ever to take my writing seriously, and wherever she may be—in graceful and contented retirement, I hope—I bless her. On Boat Race afternoons, when we all gathered to listen to the wireless, she would become very pale, savagely whispering "In— Out!" and making wild rowing motions across her desk.

She had, Miss Hudson said gently, been told about me; we could, she was sure, work something out. Her pale eyes were full of love she put her arm around me. Love, she said, was the answer. She would start praying for me right away. I was blessed.

When a fourteen-year-old gets attacked by Miss Hudson's form of religion, the attack has all the passion— though few of the compensations—of a major sexual experience. For a short while, Denis seemed very tame in comparison. *Via Crucis, Via Lucis* was my motto. A young priest commuted from Liverpool to prepare me for confirmation: he was a sunny, athletic man, who wore the three knots in the rope around his cassock, for chastity, celibacy, and poverty. Between him, and Miss Hudson, and Jesus Christ, I was in a ferment. Poetry—or rather, words— began to flood the pages of my exercise book.

> *I brought to you the intellect that I had gleaned*
> *Swiftly, haphazard, from the store of others' minds,*
> *The fine and gilded thing I had disguised so well*
> *And made believe was mine.*
> *But this you took away and, pitying,*
> *Threw to the rubbish, where it would not be despised.*

Even my father began to get worried. I was confirmed, and initiated into the mysteries of the wafer and the wine. They didn't seem particularly mysterious. By the end of the term, my Anglo-Catholic mysticism was tinged with a certain doubt:

The atom yearned for greatness. Through the air
Gliding unhurried, with determination,
Swirling precisely in a shaft of sun,
Dancing unhurried, with determination,
Onward it came to earth.

The atom settled smoothly. Things unknown,
Unthought of, with a strange, clear intuition
Entered its self, and with a secret smile
It drifted on, with strange, clear intuition,
Past the quiet evening.

Eventually, the atom ceased to be.
I read no more. The story wearied me.

It is not my intention to quote much more of this disorganized verse, which at this time filled exercise books and crawled around the margins of essays on "Intimations of Immortality" and the structure of corms. But I thought it said what I meant, even if I didn't quite know what that was. The title of the tale of the atom was "Tohu-Va-Vohu," and I've no idea what that meant, either.

My mother had two diagnoses for any untoward display of feeling: one, that I was "tired," and would feel better in the morning; the other, that it was "the reaction." It wasn't necessary for her to know what I was reacting to, or against: "It's the reaction" was a perfectly sufficient explanation.

This is how she comforted herself during my long, and somewhat turbulent reaction against Miss Hudson and God. I'm not sure what made me change my heart (my mind had very little to do with it), but hope it was something to do with distaste. Perhaps, once more, it was the Nonconformist conscience asserting itself. Miss Hudson's ecstasies, her candlelit Masses, her fervid prayers and rapt devotions, offended the Maggs in me. Anyway, I pretty soon became as passionate an agnostic as I had been a believer, and Miss Hudson mourned.

My Garden School ambitions for academic excellence had not been realized. There didn't seem to be much time for study, and in any case I suffered, in everything except English literature, from a kind of dyslexia. Figures meant absolutely nothing to me: I knew they should, and tried desperately, but why a should equal b, or why the sum of squares of the lengths of the sides of a right triangle should be equal to the square of the length of the hypotenuse, I could never tell. Latin distressed me almost as much: Nobody could explain its purpose, and no one spoke it. French seemed to make more sense, but I knew quite well, from Maurice Chevalier and from all those Nordic film stars, that a poor accent and a shaky grasp of grammar was a positive advantage in a foreign language. Science was interesting up to a point, but without mathematics it soon became as much of a mystery as everything else. History, as taught at St. Elphin's, was bunk—nothing had ever happened in the world but a dreary succession of kings and queens, wars and treaties, Picts and Scots, Whigs and Tories, all with a date attached like a price tag. Geography was much better: I loved making maps and measuring longtitude and latitude, shading the coniferous regions and areas of maximum rainfall; but geography, for some reason, was considered almost as inane a subject as Domestic Science, and I was too pigheaded to admit my enthusiasm. I excelled at Scripture, because I could write fiction, and

pounded the piano with great determination. But my
chances of passing School Certificate seemed, on the face
of it, slim.

In the meanwhile, I took up living where it had left off
with the advent of Miss Hudson. Denis wrote me short,
spidery letters with crosses on the bottom. I replied with
pages of lyrical prose. I explored the nearby Dales with my
new friend, Kay Edmunds, a chirpy, matronly little girl
from Aberystwith; we tucked our gym tunics into our
knicker legs, took off our shoes and stockings, wore our
gray felt hats at a rakish angle. I had won a packet of ten
Gold Flake cigarettes at a church fete; my father encouraged me, and I was now puffing and coughing like an
expert. I played the lead in *Berkeley Square*, trying to look
as much like Leslie Howard as possible (it was not possible). Miss Hudson got more and more desperate. In a final,
hysterical effort to bring me back to Jesus, she excommu-
nicated me from the school chapel. I could lie snug in bed
while everyone else trailed off to their devotions—"You!"
came the very faint echo of my mother's voice, "You always get what you want!"

I really thought I did. But sometimes it went wrong.
One dreary holiday afternoon, with my parents sound
asleep and Denis, I suppose, in one of his moods, I rang up
a Mr. Fox at his office. I had danced with Mr. Fox at the
Rotary Ball, to which I had accompanied my father; Mr.
Fox was at least forty-five, heavily married, and had a nasty
little black mustache. "I must see you immediately," I
breathed, trying it on. He told me to meet him at the end
of the drive in quarter of an hour. I put on a new dress,

gray wool with black stripes, cut on the cross and very (I thought) slinky. I met Mr. Fox in order to tell him my thoughts and feelings, which, in the awful silence of a vicarage afternoon, had seemed impossible to contain.

Of course that was not Mr. Fox's idea. He drove me up to a fairly deserted place called Strutt's Lane, and embraced me heartily. I didn't enjoy it at all. It was like having an old toothbrush in one's mouth. I asked him to take me home, and swore not to tell anyone.

But because Mr. Fox was now my enemy, and I was back among friends, of course I told—though only my mother. I did much more than tell: I wept and howled and demanded Denis and made such a scene that she, poor bewildered woman, must have thought I'd been raped. Since she could not bring herself to ask me what, specifically, had happened, and I was in far too much of a state to consider such trivialities, she may well have come to that conclusion. "It's the reaction," she said, and gave me an aspirin.

I was moving far into my mother's camp; my father was by now almost completely isolated, emerging only to pounce and rummage and run away again with his tail between his legs. If I were a painter, this is how I would have painted him.

Perhaps the incident with Mr. Fox made my mother realize that I was growing up. Perhaps she thought (I can hear the words) that I knew more than was good for me. In any event, we were walking around the rose garden one evening, arm in arm—our physical contacts were so rare that I think I remember most of them. Suddenly she asked,

"What do lesbians actually *do?*" It was both a proud and an awful moment, because she had asked me a question and I had no idea of the answer.

She had many loyal and affectionate lady friends, my unrelated aunts, and when she was with them she had always seemed like a stranger. Sometimes I preferred this stranger to my mother, particularly when her face flushed and crumpled into paroxysms of laughter. At the time of her question, she was having a more than usually romantic friendship with an intelligent, humorous, angular woman called Susan. My father, floundering in the shallows of psychopathology, tragically jealous, had decided (perhaps quite rightly) that his wife was a lesbian. My mother was beginning to talk to me much more, and I heard confused stories of him cutting off the light, throwing potatoes at Susan, behaving like a maniac. Certainly he arrived without warning at St. Elphin's and drove me off to a dramatic tea in Sheffield, where he threw my mother's wedding ring down on the table and told me that it was worthless, their marriage was over (he did not remember, apparently, that marriage was the coffin of love). I was extremely pleased. I thought I would enjoy life without him. When I got back to school I went straight to the Recreation Room and, probably weeping a little, confided in my friends, who were properly impressed.

Unfortunately nothing happened. My mother continued to see Susan, and to behave with uncharacteristic girlishness, laughing and blushing and singing about the place; they went on idyllic holidays to Uncle Leonard's love nest and exchanged tokens of affection and had rather interesting conversations about books and nature.

About this time, my father booked himself into a nudist colony in St. Alban's. He commanded me to go with him, and was furious when I refused. But he found nothing among the dripping trees except a group of elderly ladies dressed in spectacles, knitting scarves for their less enlightened relatives. He weighed over sixteen stone, and there was much of him to suffer. He spent one night in the chalet he had booked for three weeks, and came home. For the rest of those summer holidays he wandered naked about the shrubbery at dawn, a great, pale, disconsolate shape in the gritty light, looking as though he were searching for something.

And I, too, was jealous of Susan. It didn't seem proper that my mother should be so merry and irresponsible. I was beginning to spend a lot of time in the kitchen, chatting and gossiping, while my mother cooked. One day I was sitting on the highest rung of the kitchen steps, putting away bottled fruit in a top cupboard; my mother, down below, was prattling on about something Susan had recently said or done. I suddenly yelled, "You only think about Susan! You never think about *us!*" (or was it "me"?), and skidded down the steps and rushed out into the garden, sobbing.

Another woman might have followed me out, tried to talk to me. My mother behaved as though the incident had never happened. But Susan did ask me to tea, and sitting on the floor in front of her gas fire, in a rather untidy, collegiate kind of room, asked me sympathetic questions about my writing, and what I wanted to be when I grew up (Virginia Woolf or Ginger Rogers? I could never be sure). She didn't win me over, but I learned to put up with her.

The years between fourteen and sixteen are a lifetime; one's fifteenth year alone goes slower than a decade. September (my birthday), Christmas, Easter, the summer; and my birthday again. I was still officially in love with Denis, but it didn't seem to get very far. For a short while, my father lost his head entirely, and fell in love with me.

This was a very different situation. He mooned, wrote poetry, behaved far more like a lovesick youth than Denis did. It was not entirely unpleasant, so long as he kept his distance. I think he was dreaming of a new life, in which he could escort me to the theater and the ballet (where, God knows) and hear people say, "There goes Mr. Fletcher with his beautiful daughter, she dotes on him, you know." I think he was dreaming of becoming gentle, romantic, even protective. It was far too late. Since the night he had taken me back to St. Elphin's, my hatred of him had felt implacable.

My brother left school. One evening he championed me in an argument I was having with my father, who threw a cushion at him. I began to have a dim picture of my brother in my head, instead of in a photograph: At that time he seemed very pale, his face set in a kind of sickness or fury. I wrote poetry as though I were sweating it, covering reams of paper with damp, smudged lines. In a bus shelter in Aberystwith I read this homely verse:

When apples are ripe
They're ready for plucking,
When a girl is sixteen
She's ready for fucking.

I could hardly believe my eyes, and never told anyone, even Kay Edmunds, what I had read. I certainly felt ready for something, but couldn't put a name to it.

There were black months of studying, of avoiding Miss Hudson's recriminating eye and my father's lugubrious passion. It had been decided that in the total absence of mathematics or science, I should take botany and musical theory for my School Certificate—possibly one of them passed for a kind of science. I liked flowers and I liked music, but to dissect or analyze either seemed a waste of time. Nevertheless, I scraped through somehow. I even got honors in English literature and Scripture, though the cadences of Shakespeare and the Bible had very little effect on my style, which was remotely influenced by Céline, Dos Passos, and the lyrics of Noel Coward. Mostly, I wasn't influenced by anything but a kind of exhilarating rage. My father said I must train to be a secretary, since that was always a start; my mother said nothing. I left St. Elphin's without saying good-bye to Miss Hudson, or anybody else; and never, except in dreams, gave it a backward glance.

In the Fifth Place

1

Miss Wodge (I believe that was her name—Wodge or Warple) ran a Hostel for Girls in the Cromwell Road. From this dismal place, I traveled to the Central Educational Bureau for Women in Russell Square; and sat in front of an enormous Remington to type "The quick brown fox jumped over the lazy dog"; and struggled with Pitman's shorthand; and gave up Commercial French with no struggle at all. The loneliness of Miss Wodge's hostel was acute. I had a very small room with a divan bed, a dusty chair with wooden arms, a fumed oak bureau that was meant to turn, in some way I never discovered, into a dressing table. My parents gave me one pound a week pocket money, which arrived every Monday, safety-pinned to a letter from my mother. By Thursday, I was broke.

There was an Indian summer, and I considered whether to spend twopence on a deck chair in the park, or whether to buy some much-needed bobby pins. I decided on the deck chair. I knew nobody in London except Kay Edmunds, who lived with her family in Chiswick, where they had rhubarb pie for tea and spoke Welsh, and could seldom afford to go to Chiswick. I decided it might be a good idea to become a prostitute, though realized that since I was still a virgin I was hardly qualified for the job. I dressed carefully, put on my new lipstick, and walked through Hyde Park to Marble Arch, where there was a Lyons Corner House like a palace.

My father, on the rare occasions when he had brought me to London—once to see Colonel de Basil's Ballet Russe de Monte Carlo, which affected me deeply—had taken me to Lyons Corner House, though whether it was the one at Marble Arch or Coventry Street, I don't remember. I think they stayed open all night, and were resplendent with gilt, and strawberry sundaes. That evening I sat down at a table for two, told the waitress that I was waiting for someone, and hoped for the best.

A gentle American grandfather sat down, carefully arranging his camera, umbrella, and raincoat. He told me about his family, in Minneapolis or somewhere, and bought me a sundae. I told him how much I hated the Central Educational Bureau for Women, and that I wrote poetry. He said that his granddaughter was about my age (I had told him I was eighteen), and that if I was ever in Minneapolis, I must call by. I said that it was late, I must rush, and he said that he was glad I had friends in London.

My brother, by this time, was up at Oxford. I think Uncle Leonard had subsidized his school fees, on the understanding that he would then go into The Dairies. When my brother refused, the Maggs cut off all financial aid. But there was still a little capital left from Grandmother Nellie, and this was used to send him to Oxford. He was reading law, because the only thing he was much good at was modern languages. These paradoxes made our upbringing a puzzle.

He had attached himself to a group of Rhodes Scholars, and went with them for exotic vacations to Ibiza or the South of France. The distance between us was lessening, though almost imperceptibly. When I saw Denis in the holidays, we were both shy.

Even my parents—who had not, as far as I know, met Miss Wodge—realized that the Cromwell Road was not very desirable. They were worried by the way I stayed in my room over Christmas, writing, refusing to "join in" whatever there was to join in. I never showed my father what I wrote, but my mother didn't like it.

Perhaps I have been old and bleary-eyed,
Uncertain of my words, and feeble footed,
Aiming my foolishness at scornful children,
And waiting for my death in airless rooms.

Perhaps I faded once, a cautious spinster,
Clutching my half of life with pale defiance,
Laying my poor virginity upon the altar,
And dying soon, unfriended and unknown.

Perhaps I have been great, showering my beauty
Upon a multitude of meek adorers,
Throwing my sweeping sentences to starving stomachs
And dying wonderfully, in my youth.

There was a remarkable lack of meek adorers, and I was very healthy. It was arranged that I should go and live in Chiswick, with the Edmunds family. Nobody ever suggested that I could equally well learn to be a secretary in Derby, and live in Belper, with the Fletchers.

Chiswick was a lot better. Kay had an elder sister, Daphne, just married: I was amazed by her coiffured hair, her elegant clothes, her frivolity. There was also an older

brother, John, who was training to become a police officer.
Until he went off to barracks, or whatever trainee policemen have, we wrestled a lot on the drawing room sofa; but
he, with a mind to the law no doubt, said that we
shouldn't go to bed together until I was eighteen, and I
was greatly relieved. He took me to a roadhouse called the
Ace of Spades on the Great North Road and we danced, I
hoped, like Ginger Rogers and Fred Astaire. There was a
lot of dancing. After John left, I danced with Kay, swooping across the drawing room in a nifty palais glide.

I began to be rather frightened of boys, because there
weren't any. I made do with Kay, who was motherly and
ordinary and merry. I invented some fearful disease, for
which I said that I had to have treatment on Wednesdays:
The treatment was so extreme that it was quite impossible
for me to go to the Central Educational Bureau on
Wednesdays. With a few domestic dramas—relatives' fu-
nerals, a mother in need, a mythical sister desperate for a
visit—it was quite possible to avoid the Central Educational Bureau for at least five days a week.

But the Nonconformist was nagging again. How would I
ever be Virginia Woolf if I didn't learn something? Why
should my brother have all the education and/or fun? I
began writing the same letters I had written from the Garden School, though they may have been a mite more intelligent: I didn't want to be a secretary, I wanted to be a
writer. My father, with his usual oblique reasoning,
suggested the Royal Academy of Dramatic Art. I spurned
it—a writer or nothing. There was, it seemed, a journalism

course at University College. Somehow—God knows by
what means—I managed to get an interview with a Mr.
Solomon.

Mr. Solomon sat with one foot tucked under him in a
swivel chair, and he kept his eyes shut. He was quite encouraging. Miss Hudson had written to him that I was
undisciplined, anarchic, and a bad influence—so much for
the love of God. Mr. Solomon was quite willing to over-
look Miss Hudson's views, if I could write two acceptable
essays—one on the Art of Film, and the other I don't
remember. I wondered how he would recognize me again,
if we ever met.

My brother was very active in the Oxford Film Society,
which showed *The Battleship Potemkin* every time the
scheduled film didn't turn up. He was intimate with *The
Battleship Potemkin*. I wrote him a desperate letter, and
he responded immediately. I demonstrated to Mr. Solomon that there was nothing I didn't know about Eisen-
stein, René Clair, John Grierson, W. H. Griffiths; and was
told to enroll in the journalism course, starting the following September.

Perhaps it was my brother's support over the Art of Film
that brought us together for the first time. I don't know.
He had hated me for seventeen years, and for some of
those years I had the feeling that he had found me physically repulsive. Now, as the summer of my seventeenth
year started—green, hot, with reliable shade under trees
and awnings, like summer used to be—he took me out of a

locked box marked "sister," appraised me, decided I would do, and set me down at a Lyons Corner House table among his friends.

He must have been about twenty-two, a big, muscular young man, his hair already thinning on top—like Uncle Will, he would soon become nobly bald. His Oxford friends, already graduates of Harvard, Yale, Princeton, or Cornell, were quite a bit older. Their names sounded to me like the names of philosopher-kings: David St. Clair, John Ochs, Gregory Hartmann, Charlton Hinman. They spoke —or so it seemed to me—in the accents of Gary Cooper, Clark Gable, Cary Grant; they came from Colorado, California, Massachusetts; they were wittier, more accomplished, more glamorous, and more at ease with their glamour, than anyone I had ever met. It was the end of their last year at Oxford, and they would shortly be taking their degrees (I am convinced that all of them, except for my brother, got Firsts, Double Firsts, unimaginable honors). They asked me to go to Oxford for the ceremony.

I wore a beret on the side of my head like a plate, decorated with a huge kilt pin; a checked dress, made of rayon, I think, and cut on the cross for sveltness; a "swagger coat" of white wool; a silk scarf; and gloves to match the beret. I clutched a round scarlet handbag and a Players Medium Navy Cut cigarette. My hair was carefully brushed behind my ears, and the fringe had gone. I smiled incessantly, because I was happy and, for the first time, catastrophically in love.

It wasn't, of course, a question of who, among this dazzling galaxy of young men, I would choose (I loved them all indiscriminately)—but which of them would choose me.

Most of them lived together at 66, The High, a dark little house that for no good reason I associate with Dr. Johnson. Gregory played "Melancholy Baby" on the piano, Charlton Hinman—known as "Kadi"—played chess. David St. Clair had a visiting father, an impeccable old gentleman in a pale gray Homburg, but John Ochs and Gregory seemed to be unattached. Kadi had a formidable Dutch-American girl friend, who was going to spend the vacation bicycling around the dykes. And it was he, Charlton Joseph Kadio Hinman—who would eventually invent the "Hinman Collating Machine" for the rapid collation of Shakespeare's texts—who decided on me.

My deflowering, far from being a thing of tempestuous passion, was a carefully planned maneuver. My ignorance, he rightly decided, was appalling. First, I had to learn the theory of the thing. There were many diagrams. Next, I had to be taught about birth control: I listened with greater attention than I had ever given to botany. Finally, a Plan had to be made: It was not right to grab my virginity and run. The Plan—Kadi and my brother huddled over travel brochures and timetables—seemed to take an interminable time to make. At last it was decided that the honeymoon should take place in Jersey, halfway between home and abroad. The girl friend pedaled off and, finally, we were ready.

I can't say that, at first, I found making love much fun. I was so worried by everything I had to remember that it was more like taking a strenuous examination. Kadi said it would be all right when we got to Jersey. He packed his Plato's *Dialogues*, I bought a very sophisticated pair of blue jersey slacks with bell bottoms, I don't know what my brother packed or bought, and we set off, by way of Belper, where my parents seemed to think the whole thing was perfectly innocent and correct.

I think he was probably a very nice young man. I loved him, so it was hard to tell. We found a gimcrack little bungalow called the Blue Dragon on the cliffs overlooking St. Aubin's Bay. Kadi and I had the larger bedroom; my brother slept next door. We sprawled on the beach, got sunstroke, Kadi was beaten against the rocks by savage waves and lay, hideously wounded, on the porch sofa, grinning like a hero; Kadi and my brother played bullfights on the sand (I suppose the young were childish in those days), and chess in the evenings. We went to St. Helier and sat in a huge, domed restaurant, eating mussels while the band played "As Time Goes By." I sat on Kadi's knee on the porch, rather sulky, while he read the *Dialogues* aloud, still trying to educate me. His erudition and my frivolity had brief skirmishes: I read the *Symposium*, and he learned the words of "I've Got a Feelin' You're Foolin'." He and my brother had a long, private conversation, after which my brother went away and stayed in St. Helier, where he met a girl whose every remark was a platitude, so we called her "Ouch." I have no idea what we ate, since I couldn't cook anything but water—possibly Kadi made hamburgers and fried chicken, but I doubt it. We decided that after I had completed a year at University College, I would go to Charlottesville, Virginia, and marry him. He was due to sail back on the Bremen on August 31.

And August 31 came. I didn't think it was possible. As a child—before the Little People arrived—I used to tie myself to the end of my bed with a dressing gown cord, then order

myself to walk across the room. The fact that I couldn't
move was, I had assured myself, because I didn't *choose* to
move. It was simply a matter of will power, with which,
when I felt more inclined, I would of course dissolve the
dressing gown cord. My belief that I could walk out of
bondage—or on the water, or fly—had been nothing to my
belief that if I willed it passionately enough, August 31
would never come. But, relentless as my childish knots, we
were packing up; we were saying good-by to Ouch; we were
on the ferry to Southampton. I suppose we stayed in a
hotel, but desolation and disbelief must have blocked my
memory.

The next morning we went to the docks, and climbed
aboard the huge, grimy liner. The Dutch-American girl
friend was there, red-faced from her bicycling. I hardly noticed her. The siren blew, and my brother led me ashore.
We stood on the quay and looked high, high up, past the
crowded decks to the roof of the ship, the speck that was
Charlton Hinman, standing next to the Dutch-American.
The siren blew again, the tugs started pulling at their cables. We waved and waved. There may have been a band.
The great iron monster was slowly pulled out to sea. I
believed, at last, that I had no magic powers. It was impossible for the ship to sail; but it was sailing. I couldn't survive; but there was no such word as "can't."

2

That evening, after we had returned to London—I probably lamented the whole way—my brother walked me into

a state of complete exhaustion. My feeling is that we walked all night, but I doubt it. It was the beginning of an unequal friendship (I can't think I did anything for him) that would last at least six months—not bad, considering how transient everything seemed at that time.

We rented two very cheap bed-sitting rooms in Norfolk Square, off Praed Street. My brother had long ago turned against the law, and wanted to "get into" films. Therefore, predictably enough, he took a job hawking silk stockings. He also had to sell cosmetic gloves, called Glovelies. When the lady of the house answered her front doorbell, he was supposed to carol, "Wear Glovelies by night and have Lovelies by day!" It didn't seem a satisfactory justification for being sent to boarding school at the age of four. He spent a lot of time drawing, which he was good at. And I attended London University, in the hope of becoming a journalist when—if ever—I grew up.

It was, I think, a good course—"how to appear educated without really trying," a reasonable grounding for journalism. We took—or were supposed to take—a smattering of political theory, a swift canter through economics, philosophy, and psychology, a whirl around modern English literature; and once a week, on Tuesdays, there was a class in practical journalism, which was held in King's College and conducted by some distinguished Fleet Street hack whose name I have mercifully forgotten. For at least two months I studied as dutifully as I could, in the time left over from writing to Kadi at the University of Virginia, Charlottesville, Virginia, U.S.A. I was faithful, and even grave. My brother and I sang a good deal as we walked about Lon-

don; we bought twopenny packets of cigarettes and ate in
filthy little cafés around Paddington Station. Our parents
seemed as far away as they were.

One morning in November I received a letter from
Charlottesville: Kadi had decided to marry the Dutch-
American. It was a very long letter, but I only remember
one phrase: "I am not," he wrote, "a self-sufficient iron
man." It was raining. I didn't go to my philosophy or economics class, whatever it was that day.

I don't remember the rest of the year very clearly. There
were a lot of young men, Russian, Belgian, and (some kind
of revenge, or hope of contact?) Dutch; a couple of students from the Royal Academy of Dramatic Art, down the
street—one wore his overcoat slung around his shoulders
like an opera cloak, and carried a silver-topped cane; the
other offended me greatly by keeping a packet of French letters in the breast pocket of his navy blue blazer. There was
a subterranean club called the Blue Mask, where we used to
drink much more than was good for us; and I sometimes
took my notebook to the Café Royal, where in those days
you could still sit over a cheap cup of coffee for as long as
you wished, and scribble, and stare blankly across the huge
hall at James Agate holding small court, and tell a trouble
or two to the antique waiter. I frequently got engaged to be
married, sometimes for as long as a week, sometimes to two
people at once. My brother began to wear his Maggs
expression—stony, locked, and barred.

I had introduced him to a girl from University College, a
sultry beauty called Yvonne. We moved to new bed-sitting
rooms, Yvonne and I in the basement on one side of the

Square, my brother on the opposite side. Yvonne came from Leytonstone, and had a midget mother who sprinted in to wash Yvonne's underwear and tidy her drawers. There was no sunlight in the basement, and very little daylight either. I wrote a poem a day, without realizing that most of the time I was writing prose. Words on a page, and a pile of pages, were what mattered.

I had very soon given up Practical Journalism, realizing that what it amounted to was the simple fact that if you were reporting a fire, you did not begin your piece, "A fire broke out"; you began it, "Little Tommy Whatnot was homeless last night after fire swept the tenement building . . ." I found that I had little ambition to write about Little Tommy Whatnot's experience with fire. In any case, it seemed that was all there was, and I'd learned it. Economics and political theory went—though more gradually— the same way. I didn't, of course, think that I knew it all; I just felt sure that I would never know it at all. In the end, the only lectures I attended were on modern English literature, which were entertaining, instructive, and at least bore some relation to the way in which I misspent my time.

During that year we heard Edward's abdication speech, disembodied and sad, coming out of a blank screen in a news cinema; we didn't go to bed much over the Coronation, but fell about all night in an indoor swimming pool; Jean Harlow died, and Guernica was bombed; we read yellow-jacketed books from Gollancz's Left Book Club; and at the beginning of the summer everyone was carrying a paperback Pelican book, instant wisdom for sixpence. We revered—or pretended to revere—Auden, Spender,

Isherwood, Day-Lewis. We did revere Orwell. Auden wrote
poems for documentary films made by the General Post
Office. Most documentary films were about fishing fleets,
and sea gulls were obligatory, swooping about in gray skies
to denote the freedom, and tedium, of the fisherman's life.

In Belper, as far as I know, my mother was happy with
Susan, and my father was unhappy with everyone.

I became attached to an odd young man called Nigel,
who was trying to believe in black magic. He made many
incantations to Aphrodite, and pretended to threaten me
with an evil-looking knife. I didn't know he was pretending, and got away as fast as I could. So he drew back his
curtains and threw out the incense, and I lurched into love
again, or a form of it. A rather wild Canadian called Paul
Potts often turned up in his flat; he was helping to tear
down the Alhambra in Leicester Square, and sometimes
comforted me when Nigel's urge for a black mass became
uncontrollable. Geoffrey, Count Potocki de Montalk, pre-
tender to the throne of Poland (do I utterly malign him in
believing he came from Scarborough?), strode the Bloomsbury streets with hair and cloak billowing; in return for me
letting him use the bath in Norfolk Square (God knows
who cleaned it) he made my horoscope: It said that I
would benefit from milk, should be wary of my brother,
and that I would never achieve fame and fortune until I
wrote a play for Broadway. I believed this, since Broadway
must surely be on the way to Virginia, and even a married
professor would find it hard to resist a famous playwright. I
lived largely on such fantasies, filling in with Cadbury's
milk and nut chocolate and Woodbines.

It wasn't a healthy diet. My country childhood had been left far behind (I didn't realize that all movements on this earth are circular, and that in the end I would begin to recognize the landscape again, the wall, the bushes, the long grass path). I didn't think air, sleep, or food were necessary. So I came out in terrible boils, a Job-like quantity of boils, and was taken home to Belper, and put to bed, and was fed by my mother on milk and jelly.

Life at the vicarage had never been exactly stimulating. Now, in my convalescence, it seemed unendurable. I had no money, and had to beg and blackmail for my fare back to London. When I got there, a strange woman opened the door of Nigel's flat. He had, she said, gone to Albania. I could see the cushions I had embroidered—far from my grandmother's embroidery, to be sure—on the sofa over her shoulder. Between Albania and Virginia there seemed nothing but a vast desert of clay in which one could sink down and down among vile reptiles, punishment for selfishness and ingratitude. I sat on the top of a bus and wrote a poem.

> We, two lovers, have parted.
> We lived in Bloomsbury, we said good-by at St. Pancras.
> We went to the country once, and were together since
> January.
> Now it is June, and we have seen the last of each other,
> because summer is not our season.
> I shall associate you with discomfort, with a cold in the
> head.
> You will associate me with twopenny bus fares and boils
> in indelicate places.
> We, two lovers, have parted.
> Abelard, I apologize.

It made me feel better. It was, I felt, sophisticated and mature.

Perhaps there were a couple of hundred pounds left over from Nellie's will—the bequest seemed to stretch indefinitely—or perhaps my parents were worried about me, or perhaps my mother was even sorry for me in this new bereavement (that is improbable): Anyway, it was arranged that my father and his friend Bye should take me to Belgium for a holiday. On the way—we must have met the innocent Bye at Dover or Folkestone—we stayed the night in London, at some hotel in Bloomsbury. However sophisticated and mature I felt my poetry to be, I was still smarting from Nigel's desertion, restless after a few weeks in Belper, and longing to see my friends. My father had, without my knowledge, planned what seemed to him a delightful evening together. I told him I was going out. He was appalled (how well, now, I understand why—an evening alone in the city, abandoned, terrified). We argued. I was adamant. He gave in.

I was eighteen, no longer a child. With extraordinary stupidity—or sadism? or spiky for revenge?—I asked him to fasten my brassiere at the back. The next thing I knew, we were battling on the bed, the desperate, heavy, sickened man doing his best to rape me. I don't think I hit him. But I escaped, and finished dressing and went out, and probably had a good time. God knows how he spent his evening. We never mentioned it, and I don't think he ever touched me again, except to give me a distant kiss or a tired pat. In the past, after less violent efforts, he had often said, "Daddy shouldn't do that, should he?" sweating, pleading,

trying to make light of it. That night I think he at last believed it himself.

In Knocke-sur-Mer, my father and Bye played goff and
walked about and looked at the architecture. "Typically
continental, my dear Bye," said my father, pointing with
his stick at some fretted seaside boardinghouse. "Typically
continental." I remember very little about Bye, except the
warm, reassuring feeling that—to use his term, I'm sure—he
rather admired me. I read a letter from my father to my
mother, which said that the girls were so dazzling "that
even Peggy is extinguished." This put me on my mettle,
and gave me the courage to wear a new red satin evening
dress for the first time; it was, in its way, a success. I was
courted by a carpet manufacturer called Pierre, whom I
promised to marry, and a very handsome fellow called
Ronald Fletcher, who was a bit of a bounder because he
played goff for money. He returned to England with us. I
had enjoyed myself enormously, in spite of my broken
heart; my father hadn't, and we never saw Bye again.

We stopped in London for the night—this time at the
Regent Palace Hotel and in ominous silence. When I came
downstairs in the morning, my father was overloading a little gilt chair in the lounge: I understood why my mother
and Susan called him—behind his back—Boanerges. His
face was stormy and he appeared to weigh even more than
usual. He had been doing some sort of clumsy accounts,
and had decided that the holiday had ruined him. While
he was thundering that he would have to sell the car (a
more practical threat than suicide, but also never carried
out), I didn't attend very closely. Then he said that I must

leave the university and get a job, now, immediately, this very day. That would mean I needn't go back to Belper. I immediately read through the Situations Vacant column in the *Daily Telegraph*. By the time he left for Derbyshire that evening I was secretary to the publicity manager of Butlin's Holiday Camps and had found a room with a grand piano in Great Portland Street.

I thought it would be civil to ask my father if he would like to see this room. He agreed, reluctantly, obviously impatient to have the whole troublesome episode over. He climbed the dingy stairs, said good afternoon to various women who were hanging about the landings, looked at the room, said "Very nice," and went away. The place turned out to be a brothel, and I didn't spend much time there.

My brother was now occupied with Yvonne, and I was earning the first (it seemed, for very many years, the last) money of my life: Things had changed. The office of the Publicity Department of Butlin's Holiday Camps was in Cambridge Circus, just above the neon "White Horse" advertisement. It was a small, dingy office, and my employer seemed to suit it well. I was paid three pounds a week, and never knew quite what it was we were meant to be publicizing. My employer took me out for a drink, laid a pudgy hand on my knee, and said he was going to "exploit" me—I gathered that this meant entertaining the minor (male) film stars who made personal appearances in the Holiday Camp. I said that I was not very entertaining. That was true. I used the office typewriter to write down my fantasies:

This world—husk, grain, harvester of a world—itches in its skin; bone, skin, cranium of sky, is that too fanciful? Fanciful, oh the sweet world green in summer, idiot heads of apples on twigs, weeds ferns and marigolds all blowing, and the leaden sky enclosing us like bone gone rotten.

Go hither go thither, to and fro; or so you think. The ten toes crawl downwards into the ground, attenuated, twisting, grasping root; the rooted reeds rock hither and thither, to and fro, scraping like blades in a sink.

But what does it MEAN? It must mean something; if a meaning doesn't exist, it's necessary to invent one. The harvester, the bone, the roots and the reeds are all utter nonsense. Lead can't be like bone, bone can't be like skin, none of it can be populated by reeds and reeds have no toes and this is literature.

It wasn't publicity for Butlin's, certainly. I complained to the typewriter, consulted it, threatened it, it kept me going in the tedious, unrecognizable hours between nine and five. "In two hours and nine minutes," I told it, "I shall go home and put on my slacks and try to write and be miserable again because I can't. I think I'm giving up. I think I've got to be resigned to the fact that I'm weak—or that I just wasn't made for this sort of life. And why should I be? Only I must never be financially dependent again . . . Oh, I want nothing to do but mess about in a flat and put flowers in vases and play a piano and read about things and write balls. Be inefficiently domesticated. Be a social parasite . . . There's only one thing to do. Marry Pierre. Oh I should be so bored, so miserable. I don't want to mend his socks, I don't want to write things for him to see, I don't want to be interested in what he does . . . Anybody who was worth a pinhead would stick at this job and get a lot of satisfaction out of it. Or is that true? What's the point in sticking to this job? Butlin's Bloody Holiday Camps. Oh, a job is so much more impossible than marrying Pierre. . . ." And Oh, wailed the typewriter, Oh Oh Oh. I might have known, if I'd known myself at all, that it wouldn't last.

I think it was Ronald Fletcher (who, in spite of his sprightly goff playing, had turned out to be much older than I thought) who introduced me to Charles Dimont. I remember running with him across Piccadilly Circus, in and out of the traffic; arriving, triumphant, on the Eros island; he said, "Will you marry me?" and I said no and we set off again, perilously skidding to Lower Regent Street. As Charles was the son of a Canon, he was connected in my mind with a kind of obscure stability, a sense of home. He had a flat in Dickens' Court, off Fleet Street, which meant I could avoid the brothel for days at a time. I also knew a poet just down from Cambridge, Gavin Ewart, who had a real family—mother and father at least—in a real house, where they ate real food. My employer said he was going to Paris, and was leaving me in charge of the office. I asked Gavin to come and spend the afternoon. We were sitting innocently enough, discussing this and that profound matter, when my employer, in the best tradition of farce, walked in through the frosted-glass door. "I asked for a secretary," he squeaked, "not a bloody ornament on a Christmas tree!" I stuffed all my papers into my handbag and left, with dignity.

Gavin must have hurried back to his family, because I went alone to a café in Soho and ordered sausages and

mash. I believe the café was called the SF Grill, though I
never knew what the SF stood for. Two nuns sat opposite
me in the booth. They ate delicately and spoke quietly. I
went to the phone box and telephoned Charles. "All
right," I said. He said, "What?" I said, "I'll marry you."
He said, "Oh." I went back to the table and paid my bill
and said good-by to the nuns, who smiled as though they
liked me. That evening I moved out of the brothel and
into Dickens' Court.

It would be untrue to say that I had any clear expectations of marriage, or any positive ideas about it at all. My
parents' marriage was the only one I knew well, and it
wasn't encouraging. It's easy enough to say that I had decided that the only way I could be free and autonomous
was to depend on someone who loved me, rather than people who wanted to use me for obscure and unpleasant pur-
poses; and perhaps, in a way, that was so. But, apart from
my day on the rabbit farm, I had a very shaky understanding of freedom and autonomy; and even then, Uncle
Bertie had been in charge. It is more likely that marriage
was something I hadn't tried yet, and might prove to be a
way of "joining in"—there were more married adults, I supposed, than not; my alarming girl cousins had changed
their names long ago. Besides, I was going through all the
motions and emotions of being in love with Charles; and
in a fairly serious way, without impudence, it made a
change.

We were officially engaged for six weeks. During that
time I met his family, who seemed very safe. He met mine,

and talked intelligently to my father, who was impressed, despite himself, with the status of my prospective father-in-law. So was my mother, though the domestic arrangements in Salisbury Close were hardly up to her standards. Neither of my parents made any attempt to find out whether my fiancé was sober, industrious, virtuous, which was just as well, because I would have married him anyway. The ceremony was to take place in the Lady Chapel of Salisbury Cathedral, and I decided to dress entirely in black. Nobody protested; nobody commented at all, except the Canon, who gently remarked that the bride was black but comely. That this foolish little gesture of self-assertion might distress anyone never occurred to me. I was not informed. Therefore I did not know.

On the night before the wedding, my family and I stayed in a hotel in Salisbury. My mother and I shared a room. She was already in bed, and I was sitting staring into my own eyes in the mirror, trying to discover or answer something (the only time in my life I remember doing this —it produced a strange sensation). My mother had known about most of my love affairs, from Kadi onward; she knew that I had been living with Charles for two months. Nevertheless she said, "To think that tomorrow night you'll be sharing a bed with him—how can you bear it?" Maybe she giggled a little as she said it. Maybe she was at last trying to tell me something about herself. I found the question—if that's what it was—impossible to answer.

My father married us; that is, he did the actual "Will you take this man to be your lawful wedded husband?" and the Canon kept a firm eye on the rest. I had chosen

the hymn, without remembering the New School and my
valiant ventures. So everybody else sang, "He would valiant
be, 'gainst all disaster . . ." and Charles and I, side by side
at the altar rail, sang our own words, which were probably
mildly obscene. If my mother cried, she didn't show it.
Presumably my brother was there—he may even have been
best man—but he had receded again into his own distance,
and I forget. My father, in his no-popery white surplice and
sober stole, was ill at ease in the cathedral, though he tried
to behave well in the Close, balancing his cup and saucer
and cucumber sandwich, trying to think of something to
talk about that didn't concern God or the Church or marriage or children or the desperate unhappiness of life.

At the time, I had no idea why I insisted that we went to
stay with Uncle Bertie for half our honeymoon. In hind-
sight, it seems perfectly rational. We spent the first week or
so in lodgings at Sidmouth, because that is what my
parents-in-law had done. Then we went to Bude, where
Bertie was ushering. He took a room for us in a vast, antique hotel. It was November, cold, drenched in mist and
sea. We were the only guests, and skidded along the corri-
dors like children. Presumably we also saw Bertie, since
that was the reason for being there. I was no longer called
Fletcher, and was unfamiliar with my alias: I suppose it
was an attempt to say good-by, or to thank him for something I didn't even fully understand.

When we got back to Dickens' Court, my mother had
completely transformed the dingy, dirty flat. She must have
spent at least a week of that fortnight on her hands and
knees, scrubbing. There were a dozen comforts, and indis-

pensable objects like tea towels, wooden spoons, teapots, saucepans. As Charles had taught me how to make scrambled eggs, some of these were useful. Such hard labor, in a strange flat, alone in stranger London, may have been her form of crying.

In the Sixth Place

When life is shared with someone else, particularly a nonrelative, its quality changes. I had very seldom been entirely alone, but I had never lived with anyone, except my parents and the Daughters of the Clergy, for more than a few weeks. Married (perhaps forever?), experience was diffused: Parts of me went off with my husband, parts of me waited for him; parts of me made an attempt to mess about in a flat, put flowers in vases; parts of me wrote, and fumed, and read the life of Rimbaud; parts of me behaved quite prettily in Salisbury Close, and parts of me still felt like ringing up Mr. Fox on an empty afternoon. This is what happened to most women in those days; and does, I believe, still. Whether it is good or bad, should be accepted or remedied, is another question: It happened, it happens, and sometimes leads to a certain lackluster, a paucity of spirit, in married people.

Charles was a journalist, and had been brought up by a teetotaler father who had sometimes, out of devotion, beaten him; my husband was not very reliable. A watched telephone, I told myself with some attempt at wryness, doesn't boil. He had fantasies that he was working for, or against, the communists—the accounts were garbled, so I was not sure of anything except that when he didn't

come home on time, or three hours late, or even a whole
night late, he might be in terrible danger—bound and
gagged in some cellar, hypodermics in Carmelite Street,
chloroform in Chancery Lane? In between these mysteries,
I'm sure we enjoyed ourselves and each other. By
Christmas—with some extraordinary accuracy I had certainly never managed before—I was pregnant.

We moved out of Dickens' Court to a garden flat in a
new block in Shepherd's Bush—1, The Grampians, very
sunny, clean, and characterless. I bought a puppy from the
Battersea Dogs' Home, but it had a fit in the middle of
Shepherd's Bush Green, and had to be destroyed. My
mother came to stay, and we waited for two days for
Charles to return from some dangerous mission with the
communists or anticommunists; when he did, he was very
ill for the rest of the week. We walked through Piccadilly
Underground station on the night of my brother's birthday, March 11, and saw the posters: Hitler Invades Austria.
Within forty-eight hours, Charles had left for Vienna,
wearing a battered black trilby on the back of his head, a
cigarette clamped to his lower lip.

I followed him ten days later, flying from Crydon in a
machine like an airborne bus. It was only when I saw him
waiting at Aspern airport that I knew I was in Vienna; otherwise, I might quite possibly have stayed on the plane
until the next stop.

Reuters office was a large, dark room in our flat—Schottenring 35. There were constant parades along the broad
street—S.S., S.A., Hitler Jugend, Hitler Madchen, Pimpfe

toddling along in small brown uniforms, waving sand-castle flags. I watched from the balcony, with Anni, a buxom girl from Salzburg. Anni was our maid, and for some weeks we couldn't speak intelligibly to each other. This wasn't always necessary. On the balcony, she would say "Ah. . . !" a noise like a doting mother, and blow kisses to the strutting storm troopers. "No!" I insisted, shaking my head furiously, pounding the iron balustrade. "No! No! *Nein!*" Anni would laugh, shaking like a firm jelly, blond pigtails bobbing. She was a few months older than I and we both giggled every time she called me *gnädige Frau.*

An Austrian journalist, Hans Fischer, was working with Charles. He also worked most of the night and much of the day for the illegal Social Democrats, but we didn't know that at first. He was very handsome, and a remarkably good man—perhaps the first really good man I had ever met. He took care of us both, and tried to teach me German grammar—*der Tisch, die Türe, das Fenster; der Zucker, die Butter, das Brot.* I learned the nouns, but never their genders—there was no logic in it. My German became quite fluent, but entirely domestic. Fried potatoes were *gebratene Kartoffeln,* but mashed potatoes were *erdapfel Schmarrn*—all right, provided I didn't have to sex them. *Der/die/das Kinderwagen, Wiege, Windel, Hemd, Sicherheitsnadel*—I began to shop for the baby, which was more fun than accumulating layettes for dolls. "*Bitte, kochen Sie mir ein Ei . . . bitte, machen Sie mir das Bett . . . ist das Mittagessen fertig?*"—Anni applauded my efforts and said, "*Jawohl, gnädige Frau!*" but never, in our presence, "*Heil Hitler.*"

"23rd April 1938: It has been suggested to me by my
mother that I should write a diary. Not because I am in
myself particularly interesting, but because I am in Vienna
and should, apparently, have some Interesting Experiences.
Up to now, this hasn't occurred to me. I mean, that by
being in Vienna life is any different from what it would be
in London or, for that matter, Belper. . . ." I feel a kind
of grudging admiration for my naïveté, if that's what it
was. It would have been so easy to note down the stories
that came into the office, and pass them on to my mother
in my best handwriting; she could have sent my letters to
Aunt Jinnie, getting even.

One April evening, the three of us—myself in my wed-
ding-present fur coat—walked over the Donau Kanal to
Leopoldstadt, the Jewish district. Men and women stood
outside their shops, holding placards—"Do not buy from
Jewish pigs." The S.A. lolled about, propped each other
up, as though suffering from intolerable boredom; they
looked with disgust at the crowd, disgust at the victims. A
girl of about sixteen was made to kneel on the pavement,
stand up, kneel, stand up, kneel: The storm troopers and
the crowd stared, chewed, yawned, spat, the girl stood and
knelt. An old woman balanced on a chair, holding her placard; she had the faraway expression of an old woman
whose placard might have said "Jesus Comes" or "The
End Is Nigh" or "Moo Cow Milk Bar." We were stopped
a couple of times and told to show our papers. We had become very angry, and I was arrogant enough to show it:
"What the hell do you think you're doing? Louts!"—I fell
back on my mother's vocabulary—"Louts!" Hans took my

arm and made me walk, not too quickly, but fast enough. He looked sick. The storm troopers and the crowd shouted after us. I asked what they were shouting. Hans said, "The English people can have their ears boxed too," but it didn't sound like that to me. He made me promise never to go out without my passport; he didn't say that I had behaved like a child, and put him in danger.

So the suffering of an entire people was brought home to me, a distance of a few hundred yards. There was nothing I could do about it. Hans said that a nail in the tire of Göring's car was worth all the polemics in the world. I saved a sheaf of Low cartoons from the *Evening Standard* and pinned them around the office while Charles was out. He was furious; Reuters was meant to be unbiased. I could not be trusted with nails, so I plotted my own stubborn, if petty, resistance.

I had a favorite hat, a wide black sombrero, banded and tied under the chin with colored ribbons. With or without the hat, I looked reasonably Jewish. In an expensive restaurant we went to—now we were so rich—a group of S.S. officers took exception to my hat. They sauntered over to our table and asked me to remove it. I smiled at them, understanding perfectly. They told me to take the hat off. I smiled. One of them moved closer, to attack the hat. I weakened, and took my passport out of my handbag, pretending to look for cigarettes. They muttered and bowed and went away. It was not a triumph.

My gynecologist, Paul Singer, was Jewish. When I first went to him in March, his consulting room was a hushed place of muted browns and winking chromium, heavy magazines, dedicated receptionists. By May, he had given up the consulting room and was scurrying from place to place like a rat, never sleeping in the same bed for two consecutive nights, an ill, desperate man. He would come to see me after dark, and talked about nothing except how to get a visa, the impossibility of getting a visa. I stayed up until 4 A.M., typing his immensely long Curriculum Vitae, and later in the day, in the middle of all the trouble and worry of his life, he sent me flowers.

I ate prodigiously, and grew larger and larger. Nobody told me not to; therefore I didn't know, and voraciously devoured cream cakes, *Kaffe mit Schlag, apfel Strudel, gebratene Kartoffeln,* and *erdapfel Schmarrn.* I sang with bands in the small night clubs where we danced. In order to make room for the baby (there was room for three babies), we rented part of the adjoining flat, and knocked a door through the wall. I spent weeks perched on an unstable stepladder, painting a frieze around this enormous nursery: Three walls were decorated with German, American, and English nursery rhymes—"*Die Ganslein geh barfuss*," "East Side, West Side," and (my mother would have said, "Prophetic, alas!") "The Old Woman Who Lived in a Shoe." Around the new doorway, on the fourth wall, I painstakingly copied a Russian proverb which said, "There be four things which are little upon the earth, but they are exceeding wise . . ."—one was an ant, one a bee, but I forget the others. After we left, we heard that the Gestapo had sent decoding specialists to the nursery, where they puzzled for a long time.

As my girth increased, I felt more keenly abroad. In be-

tween the Definite and Imperfect Articles and Reflexive
Pronouns in my German exercise book, I wrote:

> I *live in Vienna.*
> *They call it Germany now.*
> *And in London the bus-conductors' hats signify*
> *That June is already half spent.*

I called it (since everything had to have a title) "Nostal-
gia," and it meant that the bus conductors would have put
white cotton covers over their hats, as they used to do.

My mother came from Belper. I had forgotten Blencathra, and was childishly excited. She stepped, small and
unruffled, off the *Orient Express,* and as I lumbered toward
her she howled, "My dear child! Are you going to have *trip-
lets?*" From then on, I didn't want to go out; pregnancy
became an illness. She had not been abroad for over thirty
years and did not know one word of German or any other
foreign tongue, but she bustled out by herself, and came
back with pudding basins, curtain material, darning wool.
Schottenring 35 became an extension of my childhood.

The games lost their interest. My mother was more
impressed by Paul Singer's inadequacy as a doctor—which
had never occurred to me—than she was by my frieze. I became lumpish as my body. "I am almost tired of it before
it arrives," I sulked to the diary intended for Interesting
Experiences. "Tired and sick to death of its clothes, its ne-
cessities, tape, cotton wool, sodaless soap, dusting powder,
long dresses versus short dresses. Before, the useless cello-
phane powder bowls and the Mickey Mouse soap were
fun. Now I just want to have it, give it to the nurse—and
recover."

Labor started a fortnight early, late at night on July 28. Charles was insensible: My mother threw cold water at him and slapped his face, probably with relish. Paul Singer was uncontactable. At the Sanatorium Auersperg, a comfortable midwife drew a picture of a steep hill, the side of a pyramid. She sat by me and marked stages on the hill, the place I had reached. I wouldn't have anesthetic, though can't remember why. After six hours, the huge child—ten and a half pounds, a great deal of her cream cake—was born. They took me up to the operating theater to stitch me up. When I first saw the baby, she was wearing a crooked purple bonnet and looked about three months old.

A week later, Hans took me to the only prize fight I have ever been to. Paul Singer had other concerns. He raced in to tell me not to feed the baby for more than six weeks, in case we got separated. My mother had no opinions about this, and jealously watched the daily nurse—a cheery, brown little woman, never known as anything but Schwester—as she strapped the baby in a version of swaddling clothes and walked her, in the shining gray Kinderwagen, in the park. But my mother scored. One morning we didn't get home until 3 A.M.; the ravenous infant had latched on to my mother's chin as she paced up and down hour after hour. My mother's chin was almost raw, and became infected. She didn't complain, but there was a glint in her eye, a satisfaction.

Hitler was demanding Czechoslovakia. There was a small war, known as German maneuvers, on the Sudeten front. My mother, worried, returned to England. Charles was away a good deal, reporting on the maneuvers and investigating Prague. I was frequently convinced that he was dead, but he always turned up again, however briefly, a bullet hole (he said) in the black trilby. Hans and Schwester took care of me and the baby; Anni's nose was put out, she flounced off to Salzburg.

It was September. Hitler had sworn he would have Czechoslovakia by October 1. His Nuremberg speech screamed through the flat, screamed through the city from dozens of public loudspeakers. Charles had been lost for a week. I went to see the British consul, a mild, circumspect man. I asked him if there was going to be a war. He smiled, and said he couldn't possibly answer that. I asked him whether I should take the baby back to England. He said that I must understand that if it was known that he was telling people to take their babies back to England, there might be panic. Yes, I said, but there *is* panic—would he advise me to go? He smiled, and said he couldn't possibly answer that. It was deadlock.

As I reached the door, he pressed the tips of his fingers together, cleared his throat, and committed himself: If he were in my position, he said, weighing the pros and cons and all things considered, he would be very inclined, yes, *very* inclined, to return to England. I thanked him very much, and ran.

Charles had temporarily surfaced in Prague. I told Schwester and the baby to meet me there in a couple of days, and took the train out of Vienna. Charles was not at the station. I took a taxi to the Alcron Hotel and found him in one of his sleeps. When he woke up, he showed me Prague. If war had broken out during those two days, I

might not have seen Madelon again for at least five years—
she suddenly had a name. At the airport I waited, sick and
subdued, for the Vienna plane. They were the last passengers, Schwester giggling and excited in her neat uniform,
her overwrapped bundle intact. We caught the London
flight with plenty of time to spare. It was easy. I sobbed
and waved through the porthole window; Charles waved
his hat. We spent that night in the Strand Palace Hotel,
where they refused to put the baby's bottle in the refrig-
erator: It was my twentieth birthday, and although I
thought I was too old to feel homesick, it felt much the
same.

The vicarage was unchanged, a bowl of windfalls on the
hall table, Michaelmas daisies, chrysanthemums, the last
weeks of September, when I had seldom before been at
home. I supposed that I wasn't at home now. My mother
turned a big room off the kitchen—originally, grandly, the
Servants' Hall?—into a place for Schwester and the baby,
whom I was slowly learning to call Madelon. Madelon
looked odd: She was very large, bald, white, bloated. Now
on her own territory, my mother took away Schwester's rice
water and substituted something wholesome, Cow and
Gate, Benger's, perhaps Frame Food. She stripped off the
baby's swaddling clothes and dressed her in matinee jackets
and leggings. I listened to news broadcasts and sat in my
apple-green bedroom writing letters to no address. My father paced up and down, urging Chamberlain to victory.

When we heard about the Munich agreement, he was almost devout: "That man," he said, "has saved my son's
life." I had to think twice before I realized that he was re-

ferring to my brother, who was now married to Yvonne
and seemed reasonably safe. However shoddy and corrupt
Chamberlain and his policy might seem in the future, my
father was one of a huge majority who believed that peace
in their time had been saved. Charles telephoned from
what sounded like the ocean bed. He said he was making
his way to Bucharest, and asked me to join him there. I
had no idea where Bucharest might be, but said I would
start immediately.

My mother was, I think, happy to see me go. In her early
sixties, she suddenly had a new baby, and a nurse to wash
the diapers and push the pram in the afternoons. There
seemed to be no danger of my settling down. "Don't
worry!" she sang, waving Madelon's lethargic hand up and
down. "All will be well!" She had made a friend of
Schwester, in spite of the language difficulties. They stood
in the driveway, waving good-by, posed as though for some
bizarre family photograph.

I don't remember anything about the journey, except
that parts of it were very frightening: We seemed to fly
over Hungary, Yugoslavia, wherever it was, at an altitude
of about a hundred feet. People in fields waved. The occasional train puffed at enormous speed straight through our
shadow. I thought that Charles might be asleep, and since
I didn't know where we were staying, this would present
problems. He was awake, at the airport, and wearing his
trilby. I expect we were both happy.

To pretend that I recall anything about those weeks, or
months—except that we ceased to be happy—would be absurd. We lived at the Hotel Splendid-Parc, which was al-

ways full of German delegates. I don't know what Charles was meant to be doing there, beyond keeping one eye on the west, the other on the east. I was ill, my just deserts for an overweight pregnancy, a fretting week in childbed, too much exertion—or so my mother explained it, after reporting every minute of the baby's development and telling me not to worry. I wasn't worried, but it did seem a little foolish to have gone through all that just to live in a hotel room in Bucharest, filing my nails and writing poetry on hotel note paper.

Charles, however, was more worried than I knew. He had been careering about the Balkans, spending large amounts of Reuters' money. They reasonably asked for expense sheets. We totted up hundreds of mythical pounds in various currencies, claiming for ladders necessary for looking over walls, for stolen cameras, for all the meals he could have eaten between Prague and Bucharest, by way of Budapest and Sofia. But he didn't have a single receipt, and even I was uneasy. It seemed necessary to get home and straighten things out.

King Carol was going to London on a state visit. I persuaded Charles that King Carol would be utterly at a loss without an English expert to advise him. Charles, with his usual plausible charm, persuaded King Carol, or at least one of his ministers. We were attached to the Royal Train, and steamed out of Romania with a fanfare of trumpets, a great deal of gold braid, and some sort of vague official position. Crossing Poland, we were shot at. The sleeping cars were not designed for astral or any other form of bodies. King Carol wore every insignia of royalty except a crown, and the food was exquisite. When we arrived at Victoria, Charles had arranged for a number of small Romanian flags to be distributed among the crowd. The plan misfired, because there was no crowd, only a posse of minor officials. I escaped as quickly as possible to Belper. The baby was four months old, and smiled politely.

We borrowed a cottage in Berkshire, and played house for a month: father, mother, baby—and Schwester to take care of us all. I was writing a novel, short stories, a poetic drama, poetry, and messages to myself: "I, author of the unfinished novel and the unfinishable poetry, a dilettante in embryo, a collection of rather bleak adolescent patch· works . . ."—it wasn't encouraging.

Even in rural Berkshire, Charles could find plots, intrigues, mysterious missions. I waited, wrapped in an eiderdown, wearing socks—it was December.

This is no night for love to walk abroad:
magic is hidden in the bole of a tree,
a diamond under the struggling root of a flower,
evil is lurking in the field paths
and in the moon.
My love, in whose veins my warm, mistaken blood is flowing,
beware of the broken bole of a tree,
the footsteps falling behind you,
the diamond you stumble upon,
beware of the field paths,
and beware of the moon, my love, as you walk abroad.

But the reality was a good deal less romantic. He resigned a split second before Reuters fired him—the receipts were still missing. We had debts, and no money.

Christmas at Belper. A Christmas tree in what was now

known as the playroom. A black winter in a bed-sitting
room in, again, Norfolk Square: making porridge on a gas
ring, stringently financed by the Canon. I tried to be a
model; the fashion magazine thought I might do for hats,
but hats, it seemed, were on their way out. I modeled for a
famous hairdresser, who cut off all my hair and, in the photographs, ironed out my nose—he paid me two pounds for
fury and distress. Everyone, except my father, seemed
happy in Belper: Madelon had grown teeth, was sitting up,
was crawling. We moved back to Shepherd's Bush, and
once more I started writing importunate letters home:
This time I didn't want to be educated, or work; I wanted
—or thought I wanted—my child.

My mother was reasonable, but firm: Surely I knew that
London was bad for babies, did I really want to deprive
Madelon of fresh air, a garden? Of course, she said, I
didn't. Now if Charles could get a job, and I could stop
smoking, and the political situation improved . . . She sent
ten shillings, and some cowslips packed in moss.

But she had forgotten that I always got what I wanted.
It took two months, but Madelon had her first birthday in
Shepherd's Bush. I boldly sent Schwester away for a holiday, but recalled her in panic twenty-four hours later:
Madelon had eaten a cigarette, been very sick, caught a
cold (or pneumonia? or worse?), had a fever. My mother
made no comment.

Hans at last left Vienna, feeling that he had done as
much as he could, and that he must now join a more official
resistance. He came to stay with us, his goodness and
strength unimpaired. I took a symbolic photograph of

Charles, or of a momentary vision of Charles: a whisky bottle wearing the black trilby, a typewriter upside down, a copy of *Das Kapital*. We were, I felt, shabby and frivolous. The outpourings were no longer romantic:

> *Have you considered mid-day things?*
> *Not those appealing to the compensatory exotic dreams of*
> > *poets*
> *living in boarding houses,*
> *but those more infinitely rare*
> *pertaining to the pleasant or unpleasant norm*
> *midway between the Ritz and a tenement building,*
> *convincing that neither is justified,*
> *yet, harder, neither should be utterly condemned.*
>
> *On this measure only should I say I love you,*
> *weighing the balance at Waterloo Station.*

Diplomats, letters, and ultimatums were flying back and forth between London and Berlin; Poland was threatened; reserves in the Army, Navy, and Air Force were called up; there were air-raid shelters, posters about gas masks, appeals for peace, promises of war. Schwester had to go home; she was about to become the enemy. We took her to Victoria, where we wept and clung, she made me promise to remember orange juice and cod-liver oil, I promised to remember, we wept, the train chugged away until the line was empty. Four hours later, she rang up from Dover, sobbing that she couldn't go, couldn't leave her schatzi. For the first time in my life, I was adult: I told her, brusquely, to go. Then I wept all night, for Schwester, for Madelon, possibly for the state of the world.

Some time before, Susan had moved from Belper to Gloucestershire. She had tuberculosis, and was dying, though very cheerfully. My mother had persuaded my father to find a living in the Cotswolds, which, unprotesting as far as I know, he did. They had moved while Schwester and Madelon were with us in London. I packed the baby, took her to Paddington, climbed on the train for Reading, Oxford (David St. Clair, John Ochs, Gregory Hartmann, Charlton Hinman, somebody else's life), Kingham, Moreton-in-Marsh, and Honeybourne. Charles was deciding whether or not to be a conscientious objector. There were a lot of women and children on the train. When we arrived at the rectory, I realized my mother was home again: There was a conservatory rioting geraniums, honeysuckle, and Virginia creeper on the soft gray stone, a mulberry tree, a village.

Sunday, September 3, was a beautiful day. My father canceled matins so that the two or three could gather together in his study and listen to Neville Chamberlain on the wireless. Neville Chamberlain declared war. They played "God Save the King," and my father stood to attention. He was fifty-nine, and momentarily looked like a young man again, ready for the fight, impatient for action, in his fantasy already winding on his puttees, polishing his leather—getting away from it all. His only uniform would be the badge and helmet and whistle of an ARP warden, and his only function in the war would be to dig for victory, getting the sugar going in his blood. I went out into the garden and stared into my daughter's pram. My mother served tea and biscuits.

Evacuees arrived in the village; there was a rumor that ten German bombers had been shot down, nobody knew where; my brother joined up as a private; Madelon walked. I couldn't bear the slow, warm days. War or no war, my parents slept in the afternoons. Hans, only mildly protesting, was interned as an enemy alien. The windfalls fell, the grass was stained with mulberries; the Michaelmas daisies flowered, and died in vases. I said I wanted to drive an ambulance, though there were no wounded, and I didn't know how to drive. My mother coaxed Madelon to stagger across the lawn. I left. In the train to London, I wrote in my notebook: "I haven't seen her grow up as a baby, and now I shan't see her grow up as a child." It was a fact, rather than a complaint. I looked out of the window at Moreton-in-Marsh, Kingham, Oxford, Reading, and thought about other things.

Two days later, it was my twenty-first birthday. My brother and Yvonne, Charles and I, rich on birthday checks, went to the Café de Paris in Leicester Square. We couldn't afford a table by the dance floor, so sat in the balcony. We said it was like a scene from *Cavalcade*. Beautiful officers in decorative uniforms danced with women dressed in satin and gold lamé; colored spotlights swept the room, yellow, red, or blue dancers, yellow, red, or blue waiters with their trays held high; the saxophonists stood up in a platoon, their eyeglasses twinkling. A blond girl sat at the piano and sang. Somebody said her name was Hildegarde. She sang cheekily, pounding the keys:

We're gonna hang out our washing on the Siegfried Line,
Have you any dirty washing, mother dear . . .

We drank champagne to the present and the future, but not to the past that I have tried to celebrate here.